Historical American Biographies

BENJAMIN FRANKLIN

Founding Father and Inventor

Leila Merrell Foster

Enslow Publishers, Inc.

40 Industrial Road
Box 398
Berkeley Heights, NJ 07922
USA

PO Box 38
Aldershot
Hants GU12 6BP
UK

http://www.enslow.com

Library of Congress Cataloging-in-Publication Data

Foster, Leila Merrell.
Benjamin Franklin, founding father and inventor / Leila Merrell Foster.
p. cm. — (Historical American biographies)
Includes bibliographical references and index.
Summary: Discusses the life of the multi-talented American who was a scientist and an inventor, a writer and a printer, as well as playing an influential role in the early history of the United States.
ISBN 0-89490-784-0
1. Franklin, Benjamin, 1706-1790—Juvenile literature.
2. Statesmen—United States—Biography—Juvenile literature.
3. Inventors—United States—Biography—Juvenile literature.
4. Scientists—United States—Biography—Juvenile literature.
5. Printers—United States—Biography—Juvenile literature.
[1. Franklin, Benjamin, 1706–1790. 2. Statesmen. 3. Printers.
4. Scientists.] I. Title. II. Series.
E302.6.F8F724 1997
973.3'092—dc21
[B] 96-45313
CIP
AC

Printed in the United States of America

10 9 8 7 6 5 4 3

Illustration Credits: Department of the Treasury, Bureau of Engraving and Printing, p. 115; Library of Congress, pp. 7, 12, 23, 24, 48, 52, 56, 63, 66, 68, 71, 77, 82, 88, 95, 101, 103; Independence National Historical Park Collection, pp. 14, 34, 108, 114; Stephen Klimek, pp. 58, 73.

Cover Illustration: © Corel Corporation (background); Library of Congress (inset).

Contents

1

Creating the United States

John Hancock warned his fellow members of the Continental Congress which met in Philadelphia in 1776, "There must be no pulling different ways; we must all hang together." These men had just declared the independence of the American colonies from Great Britain.

Benjamin Franklin, then seventy years old and the oldest member present, agreed, "We must, indeed, all hang together, or most assuredly we shall all hang separately."[1]

Franklin had come up with a play on words that expressed the seriousness of what they had just done. They had agreed to sign the Declaration of Independence. This paper contained a list of the reasons why they felt the colonies had to break free from Great Britain, the country that governed them. The last sentence read, "And for the support of this declaration, with a firm reliance on the protection of Divine Providence, we mutually pledge to each other our lives, our fortunes and our sacred honor."[2]

While the first record of this story was not produced until years after Franklin's death, the account rings true. Great Britain would consider these leaders traitors. If Britain had won the Revolutionary War, death would have been the most likely punishment for signing such a document. Indeed, the topic of hanging came up in other discussions. Benjamin Harrison of Virginia, a heavy man, joked that he would have a more merciful hanging because his neck would be broken at once, whereas the slimmer Elbridge Gerry of Massachusetts, might be left dangling for some time.[3]

Why Franklin Signed the Declaration of Independence

What possessed a practical man like Benjamin Franklin to risk so much? He was at the peak of his career. Franklin was famous for his writing. His *Poor Richard's Almanac* was a best-seller. He was recognized as a scientist for his work with lightning and electricity. Franklin had been elected to the Royal Society, an important group of scholars in England. Americans liked his many inventions, such as the Franklin stove and the lightning rod. He had been given honorary degrees from Harvard and Yale in America, St. Andrews University in Scotland, and Oxford in England. He was probably the most famous of the signers of the Declaration.

Franklin knew firsthand the risk he took in signing the Declaration. He had just come from England. There, he had tried to find some way of lifting the tax burdens that Britain had placed on the colonies. He saw the positions of the English and the colonists hardening. Compromise seemed beyond reach. He was fed up with the king and with the people who ruled the colonies from England. His ideas were summed up in the words that he

This picture shows what it must have been like when Franklin signed the Declaration of Independence in 1776. Other members of the Continental Congress look on.

chose for the seal of this country: "Rebellion to tyranny is obedience to God."[4]

Tyranny is a strong word. It means the oppressive and unjust rule of another. Franklin asserted that it is all right to rebel, to fight against such rule. Britain was treating the colonies as a parent might deal with his or her children. It was called the "mother country." The rulers in Britain believed they knew best what the colonies needed. King George III of Great Britain ruled with the belief that God had chosen him to be king. The signers of the Declaration were willing to fight to get out from under his rule. They felt that their actions were all right with God. However, they knew that others would not agree with them unless they could persuade them with their reasons.

The Conflict Between Britain and the Colonies

How had this conflict come about? When people first left Britain and sailed to the New World, they needed the support of their native countries. They were used to things that were not available in the new land. People had to learn how to settle and clear the land so that they could produce food and other necessary supplies. They depended on the mother country.

As the colonists eventually learned how to do and make what they needed, they did not need to buy so much from abroad. In fighting and defending themselves against the French and the Native Americans who attacked them, the colonists developed leaders. They had proved themselves by carving out a life for themselves in a new land. Visitors from Europe were treated well, but they reported that the colonists were a proud and independent people.

On the other hand, back in Great Britain some leaders thought of the colonies only in terms of their value to the mother country. After all, Britain had explored and settled this new land. It had put money into it and was defending it against others. The British felt that it was only right to tax the colonists to get some of their money back.

The colonists did not agree. They tried to get the British to see that the taxes were too much of a burden. However, the British only tried harder to get the money that they demanded. They allowed their officials to use search warrants to find out whether the taxes were being paid on goods brought into the colonies. The colonists resented the officials who snooped around their buildings. In fact, many bought and sold goods without paying the tax.

Then the British tried to tax business inside the colonies. They issued stamps that had to be put on newspapers, legal papers, ship's papers, and even on playing cards. The British felt that this tax was a fair way to cover the cost of their army and navy in the

The Thirteen Colonies

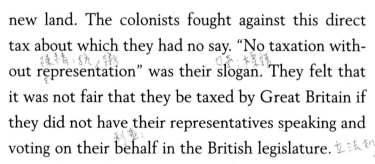

It is hard to know what to call the thirteen colonies before the Declaration of Independence was adopted and they became the United States. Britain had other colonies, such as Canada, in the New World. "American colonies" in this book means the thirteen that provided signers of the Declaration of Independence: New Hampshire, Massachusetts, Rhode Island, Connecticut, New York, New Jersey, Pennsylvania, Delaware, Maryland, Virginia, North Carolina, South Carolina, and Georgia.

new land. The colonists fought against this direct tax about which they had no say. "No taxation without representation" was their slogan. They felt that it was not fair that they be taxed by Great Britain if they did not have their representatives speaking and voting on their behalf in the British legislature.

Leaders of Massachusetts and Virginia spoke out against Britain's actions. The angry colonists formed mobs. The British met the action of the mobs with force. In Boston, five people were killed in what became known as the Boston Massacre. The British taxed more goods—tea this time. One night in 1773, a group of colonists protesting the tax on tea dressed up like Native Americans. They boarded three tea ships in Boston Harbor and dumped the tea into the water, calling it the Boston Tea Party.

Finally, the leaders of various colonies met together in 1774. They discussed what could be done to make Britain loosen her control and allow them more freedom. The king and the British refused to comply with their requests. In March 1775, in Virginia, Patrick Henry made his "Give me liberty or give me death" speech. In April in Massachusetts, farmers fired the first shots against a British force that was marching to seize ammunition and colonial leaders.

How the Continental Congress Acted

By the time people from each of the thirteen American colonies met in the Second Continental Congress, Franklin was home from England. He was elected a delegate from Pennsylvania to this body. The king was so angry with the claims of the colonists that he denounced them as rebels. By this time, it was becoming more and more obvious to the colonists that there was little hope that they could talk their way into relief. They would have to be ready to fight. Congressman Richard Henry Lee of Virginia moved that the United Colonies should be free. On July 2, 1776, most of the members of Congress agreed. The Congress formed a committee to write the document that would announce to the world that a new nation had been born.

Benjamin Franklin discusses the Declaration of Independence with other members of the committee: Thomas Jefferson, John Adams, Robert R. Livingston, and Roger Sherman.

The committee met to discuss the contents and then turned the writing of the paper over to Thomas Jefferson. A skilled writer though only thirty-three years old then, Jefferson was chosen to draft the paper because he represented Virginia, the largest colony and the one whose delegates had proposed the resolution for independence. It has been said that if Franklin had written the Declaration of Independence, with his wit, he would have included a joke.[5]

After Jefferson had finished his draft, he sought the advice of Franklin and John Adams, both members of the committee. Franklin suggested a few changes in the wording. Then after committee approval, the Declaration went to the Congress for debate. Jefferson sat quietly and let others defend the document.

Franklin noticed how hard it was for Jefferson to listen to all the changes being discussed. So, at the meeting Franklin told the story of a friend who had composed a sign for a man who was about to open a shop to sell hats. The friend wrote, "John Thompson, Hatter, makes and sells hats for ready money." Then he drew a picture of a hat. The first person he showed the sign to suggested dropping the word "Hatter" as unnecessary. The second person told him to strike "makes" because people would not care who made the hats. The third wanted the phrase "for ready money" dropped. Sales were

The Liberty Bell that rang when the Declaration was approved is still in Philadelphia. On it are words from the Bible: "Proclaim liberty throughout the land unto all the inhabitants thereof."

not to be made for credit anyhow. The fourth eliminated "sells hats" since the shopkeeper would not give them away. The sign maker was left with "John Thompson" and a picture of a hat. The Declaration of Independence escaped such drastic changes. Jefferson remembered Franklin's kindness in easing his tension at the meeting by telling the story.[6]

On July 4, 1776, the members of the Congress approved the Declaration of Independence. A bellman had climbed the steeple of the meetinghouse that morning. People expected the Congress to come out with some sort of statement about independence. The man waited to ring the bell until he had a signal from a boy down below. When the boy clapped his hands and shouted, the man rang the bell. Engraved on this Liberty Bell was a quotation from the Bible: "Proclaim liberty throughout all the land unto all the inhabitants thereof."

Not all the colonists were in favor of the action taken by Congress. Franklin was challenged by a young man who had been seen to be drinking a good deal of rum, "Aw, them words don't mean nothing at all." Always quick with a good comeback, Franklin replied, "My friend, the declaration only guarantees the American people the right to pursue happiness. You have to catch it yourself!"[7]

2

Growing Up Independent

What kind of a childhood did Benjamin Franklin, who was so important to the creation of our country, have? We know a great deal about his family and childhood. Franklin wrote his autobiography, the story of his life for his son. His book is an account of his actions to about 1757. After that, we have to depend on his letters and the accounts of other people to piece together Franklin's life.

Franklin's Family

Franklin was proud of his family and traced its history back to English roots. He was the youngest son of the youngest son for five generations back. Because a family's land usually went to the eldest son, younger sons had to make their own way in the world.

His family was Protestant since the time the Protestant faith began in England. Even when Queen Mary I attacked Protestants during her rule of England, Franklin's ancestors held to their beliefs. Franklin tells how his great-great-grandfather used to read a Bible when it was against the law to do so. The book was strapped under the cover of a footstool. One of the children stood guard at the door. If an officer came, the child gave the alarm. His great-great-grandfather would then turn the footstool over, hiding the Bible on the underside. That way he would not be caught.

Franklin's father, Josiah, decided to leave England for America, in order to have more freedom to worship. He brought his wife, Anne, and three children, Elizabeth, Samuel, and Hannah, to the Boston area in 1683. With Anne, Josiah had four more children, Josiah, Anne, Joseph (who lived five days after birth), and Joseph (who survived only fifteen days). After his wife died, Josiah Franklin remarried and had ten children with Abiah Folger. These children were named John, Peter, Mary, James, Sarah, Ebenezer, Thomas, Benjamin, Lydia, and Jane. Although the older children had grown up and left home before the younger ones were born, Ben could remember thirteen of these children sitting at his father's table at one time.

Franklin's Childhood

Benjamin Franklin was born on January 17, 1706, the youngest son, with two younger sisters. He joked that he was in church all day when he was born. His mother had been at service in the morning. Then she gave birth to him. He was baptized that afternoon.[1]

One story that Franklin remembered was when he was seven and had been given some money. He headed right to the toy shop but bought a whistle from a boy he met on the way. At home he blew his new toy so much that no one liked the whistle. They told him he had paid too much for the toy and that he could have bought many other things with the same sum. They teased him so much that he grew to hate the whistle.[2]

In those days, boys learned a trade by working for others. Josiah Franklin arranged for each of his sons to learn a different job. He thought Ben would become a minister. Since Ben had learned to read at an early age, his father sent him to school when he was eight years old. The school trained boys to be ministers.

Ben was a quick learner. He started out in the middle of his class but soon rose to the top. He was even sent ahead to the next grade. However, Josiah Franklin took his son out of that school after a little less than a year. He told his friends that he could not afford to send Ben on to the university because he had to support a large family. Also, he said that ministers did not earn much in spite of all their schooling.

Instead, Ben was sent to a man who taught writing and arithmetic. Ben was great at writing but had problems with math. After Ben had only about two years of school, Josiah took him home to learn his trade of making candles and soap.

Ten-year-old Ben did not like the work. He wanted to be a sailor on ships like those he saw in Boston Harbor. Since Ben's older brother left home to become a sailor, his father objected to Ben pursuing the same lifestyle. But because of his interest, Ben learned very young how to swim and manage boats.

Ben also enjoyed fishing with his friends. He usually was the leader of his gang. Once he got them all into trouble. They used to fish for minnows on the edge of a salt marsh where it was very muddy. Nearby they found some stones that were to be used in a new house being built. Ben suggested to his friends that they use the stones to build a wharf so that they would not have to stand in the mud.

The gang agreed. They showed up at night and took the stones for their project. The next day, the builders of the house noticed the missing stones. They hunted for them and found out who had taken them. Ben and his friends were punished by their parents. Ben argued that the project was good. However, he came to agree with his father that "nothing was useful which was not honest."[3]

Ben respected his father. Josiah Franklin could draw and play the violin. He was skilled with his hands. Others came to him for advice. Often he would invite a friend for dinner. They would talk about things so that his children could listen to the discussion and learn. Ben often cared more for what was being said than the food he was eating.

After two years of working at his father's shop, Ben still disliked his job. His father, fearing that his son might run away to sea, tried to help Ben find different work. He took Ben on walks with him to see if there was some other trade he might like more. Ben learned how to do many jobs from those walks as he watched others at work. Later he applied his experience. He could do small jobs around the house and build things to test his theories in science.

Printer

At last, the family decided that Ben should go to work for his older brother James. James was a printer and had set up his shop in Boston. Ben liked the idea of printing better than making candles and

Benjamin Franklin's Tribute to His Parents

Benjamin Franklin's father died at the age of eighty-nine; his mother, at eighty-five. Franklin had these words placed on their gravestone in Boston:

Josiah Franklin,
and
Abiah his wife,
lie here interred [buried].
They lived lovingly together in wedlock
fifty-five years.
Without an estate, or any gainful employment,
By constant labor and industry,
with God's blessing,
They maintained a large family
comfortably,
and brought up thirteen children
and seven grandchildren
reputably.
From this instance, reader,
Be encouraged to diligence in thy calling,
And distrust not Providence.
He was a pious and prudent man;
She, a discreet and virtuous woman.
Their youngest son,
In filial regard to their memory,
Places this stone.[4]

soap. At that time, it was the custom to have spent a number of years under a contract to learn a trade. This practice was called an apprenticeship. Ben did not like the idea of signing up to work for his brother. He had to promise to stay for nine years, until he was twenty-one years old. He would not receive real wages until his last year of the contract. However, he agreed to the contract in order to get away from the candle and soap trade.

One benefit of this new trade was that Ben would have access to good books. He could borrow books from booksellers in the evening if he returned them the next morning. Often he would stay up at night reading.

Around this time, Ben began writing poetry. He even had his brother print up some of his poems, which Ben sold on the streets. His father was not pleased, because poets were often poor. Ben turned to prose writing, which does not depend on rhymes or meter, and was to be of greater use to him.

Ben also liked to debate his friend, John Collins. The two wrote letters to each other. For example, John thought women should not be educated. Ben took the opposite view. Ben also wrote down arguments that he read in other books. This practice helped him to learn new words and organize his thoughts on paper.

He used to write his name in a fancy way. Once

Ben Franklin's signature.

an older man saw it and said, "What fool's name is this?"[5] After that, Ben wrote his name in a plain and simple way.

When Ben was about sixteen, he decided to become a vegetarian. He had convinced James to give him half the money being spent to house and feed him. He was tired of being teased about what he ate, so he bought his own food. Then he used some of the money to buy more books. Also, by getting his own meals and eating by himself, Ben had more time for reading.

Conflict with a Brother

James Franklin began to print one of the earliest newspapers in America, the *New England Courant.* Ben sold the papers on the street. Some of James's friends began writing for the paper. Ben wanted to do the same, but he thought his brother would not print anything he had written. So he wrote a number of stories that were supposed to have been authored by a woman, Silence Dogood. Then one night he put one of his stories under the door of the shop.

The story was found and printed. James's friends praised the story, much to Ben's delight. Ben continued to write under the name of Silence Dogood. Dogood poked fun at what "she" saw in Boston. She even argued in favor of schooling for women.

When Ben ran out of ideas for the stories, he told his brother who wrote the pieces. James was not pleased to have been fooled by his brother. However, the other writers thought highly of Ben's stories.

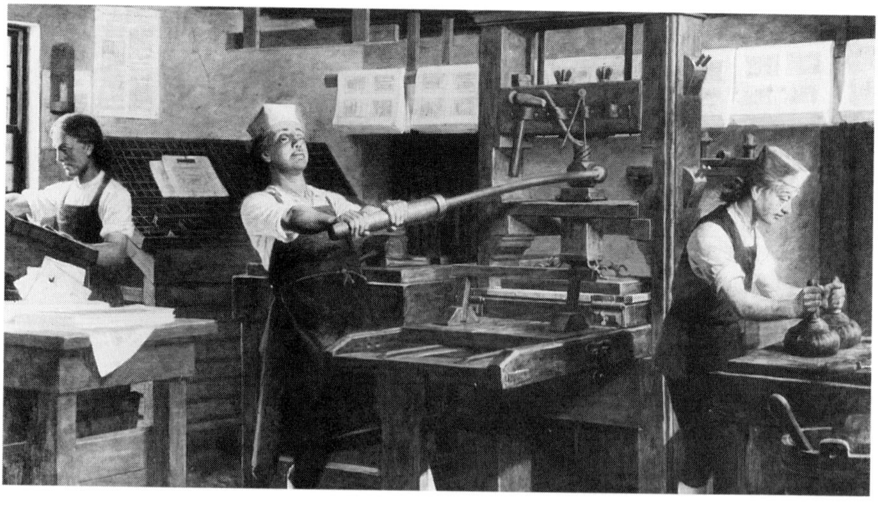

Ben Franklin became a printer. He learned the trade in the shop of his brother, James. Franklin loved to read and started to write stories for the newspaper that James printed.

James's Influence on Ben

Benjamin Franklin wrote that his brother James's "harsh and tyrannical treatment of me might be a means of impressing me with that aversion to arbitrary power that has stuck to me through my whole life."[6] In other words, James's actions made Ben value independence.

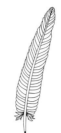

Ben felt that this joke might have been one cause of the problems he had with James. James treated Ben like any other worker—not as a brother. James often beat Ben and loaded him with work. Many times the brothers asked their father to be the judge of their disputes. Ben usually won.

Because of his brother's treatment, Ben wanted out of his apprenticeship with James. He had the chance when James was put in prison for a month because of a political story printed in his newspaper. In those days, people could be jailed for writing against their leaders. Instead of leaving, Ben ran the paper while James was away. He wrote some jabs at the people who had put his brother in jail. When James was set free, he was told that he could no longer print the paper. To get around this order, the paper was put out under Ben's name. For Ben to run the paper, the old contract had to be torn up. Still, Ben had to sign a new contract with James for the remainder of his time of service. This new contract was to be kept secret.

When Ben decided to leave, James could not reveal their secret contract without getting into trouble with the law. But he did prevent Ben from getting a job as a printer in Boston by talking with his friends. This time their father sided with James against Ben.

Ben was just seventeen. He knew that the leaders in Boston did not like some of the things he had written when he ran the paper. Many objected to his views on religion. They thought that he did not believe in God, or not in their God at any rate. Ben decided that it was time to leave Boston.

He had his friend Collins book a place on a ship heading to New York City. Collins told the captain that his friend had to leave town in secret because he had gotten a girl pregnant. Otherwise the girl's relatives might force his friend to marry her. Ben sold some of his books to pay for his trip and was taken on board privately. With very little money and with no letters of introduction to others, he secretly left Boston.

3

Running Away and Coming Home

Seventeen-year-old Franklin landed in New York City three days after leaving Boston. He was three hundred miles from home. He did not know anyone there and had very little money. He might have become a sailor then; however, by this time he was proud of his skill as a printer and wanted to work at this trade.

Travel to Philadelphia

On this trip, Franklin abandoned his vegetarian diet. He watched many codfish being caught and cut open and saw that the bigger fish had eaten smaller ones. He loved to eat fish and thought to himself, "If you eat one another, I don't see why we may n't eat you."[1] He remarked that this was an example of finding a reason for everything you want to do.

Franklin tried to get a job in New York with a man who had been a printer in Pennsylvania. The man could not give him any work. He told him that his son, a printer in Philadelphia, Pennsylvania, might have a job to offer him. Philadelphia was one hundred miles away from New York. How Franklin got to Philadelphia is an indication of how difficult travel could be in those days.

Franklin wore his working clothes and stuffed extra shirts and stockings in his pockets. He sent a chest of his best clothes to follow by sea. Then he found a boat that would carry him across the bay to Amboy, New Jersey. A storm tore the rotten sails to pieces. One person fell overboard. The surf was so rough they could not land. Franklin tried to sleep, but the spray soaked him. They had spent thirty hours on the boat without food and with little to drink. That evening in Amboy, Franklin came down with a fever. Feeling better the next morning, he pushed on.

He was told that if he could get to Burlington, New Jersey, he would find boats that could take him to Philadelphia. Burlington was fifty miles away. Franklin set out on foot, but it rained very hard, and he was tired, so he stopped at an inn. People at the inn where he stayed thought he might have been a runaway servant because of his clothes. He was afraid he might be arrested because he broke the job contract with his brother.[2] Franklin admitted that he was "beginning now to wish that I had never left home."[3]

The next morning he set out and made it to within eight or ten miles of Burlington. The inn that he stayed at this time was run by a man who was friendly. The next day—Saturday—he made it to Burlington. There he learned that the boats for Philadelphia had just left. He would have to wait until Tuesday for the next boat. Franklin went back to a woman who had sold him some gingerbread and asked her advice. She invited him to stay with her. However, he discovered that another boat was headed to Philadelphia that evening.

Newcomer

The people on that boat let Franklin join them. They all had to row because there was no wind to fill the sails. By midnight, some thought that they had passed the city. They pulled into shore and set up camp. They made a fire with some fence rails and stayed overnight. The next morning, they saw Philadelphia.

In dirty working clothes, tired from the rowing, and hungry, Ben Franklin landed in the city of Philadelphia. He had little money left but went to a bakery to buy bread. He asked for two kinds of cheap bread but was told that they did not have them in that city. He asked for three pennies worth of whatever kind of bread they did have. He ended up with three rolls.

Since his pockets were stuffed with clothes, he put one roll under each arm and ate the third. When he walked past the house where his future wife, Deborah Read, was standing, she thought he looked silly. He went on to the river where the boat he had come on was docked. He gave his other two rolls to two former fellow passengers, a woman and child, who were waiting to continue their journey on the boat.

It was a Sunday in October 1723, so Franklin joined a group of people going to the great meeting house of the Quakers. The Quakers are a religious group, also known as the Society of Friends, that settled in Pennsylvania. They value silence in their worship. During the service, Franklin promptly fell asleep and did not wake up until someone roused him at the end.

Franklin still needed to find a place to stay. Seeing a young Quaker man he thought he could trust, he asked about the inns. The man steered him away from a bad one to a better place. When he was eating dinner there, some people again questioned him. Was he a runaway servant? After all, he was young and dressed in working clothes. He went to bed early and the next morning was ready to see about finding a job.

When he came to Andrew Bradford's print shop—the one that he was looking for, he discovered that the printer's father had come by horse from New York and arrived at his son's place before Franklin. The son did not have work, but the father took him to another printer, Samuel Keimer. Keimer gave Franklin a job.

Franklin did not think highly of the two printers. One could not read. The other knew nothing about the presses. Keimer had no furniture, so he could not offer Franklin a place to stay. Bradford offered Franklin a room and help in obtaining odd jobs. However, Keimer did not like Franklin's staying at the home of his competitor. Therefore, he arranged for his new worker to live at the home of John Read, Deborah Read's father. By that time, the chest with Franklin's better clothes had arrived. This time Deborah Read had a better impression of Franklin than when she first saw him with the rolls.

Franklin began making a new start in Philadelphia. He made friends with a group of young people who liked to read and spent his evenings with them. He spent little of the money he earned. Franklin tried to forget Boston. Only his friend Collins knew where he was, and he kept it secret. The secret came out when his brother-in-law,

Robert Holmes, heard that Franklin was in Philadelphia. Holmes was master of a ship that traveled between Boston and Delaware, and this information reached him at a stop in Newcastle, Delaware.

Befriended By the Governor

Holmes wrote a letter to Franklin telling him of the concern of his friends in Boston and urging him to return. Franklin replied, explaining the reasons he had left. When Holmes received the letter, the governor of Pennsylvania, Sir William Keith, was with him. Holmes showed Keith the letter. Keith was surprised to learn how young Franklin was. He thought the eighteen-year-old showed great promise. He told Holmes that Franklin should set up shop on his own in Philadelphia.

Later Keith, with a friend, Colonel French, visited Franklin. They told him that if he set up a shop, they would try to send him public business. Franklin said that he did not think his father would give him any money to buy what he needed for a print shop. The governor said he would write a letter to Franklin's father encouraging him to give his son the money.

So the next year, in April 1724, Franklin boarded a little ship for Boston. He left his job, telling his boss that he was going to visit his friends. He took the letter from the governor to his father with him.

During the stormy trip, the ship sprang a leak, and Franklin and the other passengers had to keep pumping out water to avoid sinking.

Franklin's arrival in Boston seven months after he had left was a total surprise to his family. His brother-in-law Holmes had not written about him. His family, except for James, welcomed him. Franklin went to James's print shop. He was better dressed than when he had left. He had money in his pocket. James looked at him and turned back to his work. The other workers crowded around Franklin with questions. When Franklin left, he gave the others a coin so that they could buy a drink. James was angry. He felt his brother had insulted him before his workers by showing off his money and good fortune.

Franklin's father was surprised at the governor's letter. He waited for Holmes to return to Boston to ask what kind of a man the governor was. Holmes tried to speak up for Franklin. However, Josiah Franklin thought that his son was just not old enough to manage such a shop. The cost of the machines was very high. He finally decided not to give him the money and wrote a letter to the governor stating that he felt his son was too young for such a job.

Still Josiah Franklin was pleased that his son had friends who thought so highly of him. He agreed to let his son return to Philadelphia and told him to save up his money. If he came close to the needed amount by the time he was twenty-one, his father would help him out with the rest.

On the return trip, Franklin made friends with two young women and an older Quaker woman on the boat. The older lady warned him to avoid the two younger women. Franklin later learned that she was right—the two young women stole silver spoons from the captain and were punished.

Franklin began to have problems with his friend Collins. Collins had decided to join Franklin in Philadelphia, but he took up drinking brandy and

The east view of Philadelphia at the time Franklin lived there shows that the city was a busy port.

gambling. He borrowed a lot of money from Franklin, which he never repaid. Collins later moved to Barbados in the West Indies, where he became a teacher. He promised to repay his debt to Franklin, but he never did.

Back in Philadelphia, the governor said he would set Franklin up in a print shop. He told Franklin to make out a list of what he would need from England, and he would send for the items. Franklin thought very highly of Governor Keith. He brought the list to the governor, who suggested that Franklin go to England to pick out the necessary machinery, such as a press and types, and to make contacts for selling books.

Since there were not many ships traveling between London and Philadelphia, Franklin kept working for his old boss. He kept secret the plans to set up his own shop. He also courted Deborah Read. However, since they were both just eighteen years old, her mother thought it would be better for them to wait to get married until Franklin returned from England and set up his shop.

On to London

When the ship for England was ready to sail, Franklin went to the governor to collect the letters of introduction and credit he had promised. Several times Franklin was told that the governor was busy but would send them along later. The governor's aide told him the letters would be put on board his ship and wished him a good trip.

Franklin was puzzled but did not doubt that he would receive the letters. Without them, no one would give him the equipment he needed. Colonel French boarded the ship and gave the captain some letters from the governor. When Franklin asked for his mail, the captain told him that all the letters had been put in one bag, and he could not sort them then. However, there would be time before they landed.

When they were close to England, the captain let Franklin look over the mail. Franklin found no letters addressed to him. He picked out two that appeared, from the handwriting, to be from the governor's office and were addressed to a printer and a paper seller. He planned to deliver these himself.

Franklin made his way to the paper seller first. Franklin gave him the letter that he thought was from the governor. The paper seller said that he did not know the governor. When he opened the letter, he remarked: "O! this is from Riddlesden. I have lately found him to be a complete rascal, and I will have nothing to do with him, nor receive any letters from him."[4] It was not the letter Franklin hoped it was.

What was Franklin to do? He was in England without the promised money to buy printing supplies. He sought out a friend he had made on the ship coming over. Thomas Denham was a merchant from Pennsylvania. Franklin told him what had happened. Denham advised Franklin that Governor Keith had no funds to give to others for he had little money himself. He told Franklin that the governor could not be depended on and probably had never written any letters. Denham suggested that Franklin work for some printers in England. "Among the printers here, you will improve yourself, and when you return to America, you will set up to greater advantage."[5]

Franklin did gain from the letter from Riddlesden. It told of a scheme against a lawyer from Philadelphia who was a friend of Denham. When the lawyer arrived in London, Franklin gave him the letter. The lawyer was glad to know what it contained and became Franklin's friend.

Franklin's feelings toward the governor changed, however. He felt that the governor made promises he could not keep just to please people. He gave false hope. Yet Franklin felt that the man was sensible in other ways. Some of the best laws were passed when he was in power.[6]

Living in England

James Ralph, another of Franklin's friends, had come over on the ship with Franklin. Ralph was supposed to be traveling to England to obtain goods to sell in America. However, once in England, Ralph told Franklin that he was leaving America forever.

He was running away from his wife and child because he did not like his wife's family. Ralph had brought no money with him because he had just enough to pay for the trip to England. He was another friend who borrowed money from Franklin and never repaid it.

Franklin found work at a print shop. He and Ralph spent a good deal of money on plays and other pastimes. Because of these expenses, Franklin did not keep enough of his pay to be able to return to America. He wrote only one letter to Deborah Read to let her know that he was not likely to be able to return soon. Franklin later admitted that he regretted not having written more letters to her.[7]

As he did in Philadelphia, Franklin made friends easily in England. He borrowed books from a bookseller next door to his workplace and read a great deal. While in England, he wanted to meet Sir Isaac Newton, the scientist, but never did.[8] However, he did go to see Sir Hans Sloane. Sloane had a collection of curiosities and specimens of natural history that were to form the start of the British Museum. Franklin owned a purse made of asbestos to protect against fire. He wrote to Sloane about his purse and was invited to Sloane's home. According to Franklin, Sloane persuaded him to sell the purse to Sloane for his collection, "for which he paid me handsomely."[9]

Franklin moved to a larger printing shop, which employed nearly fifty workers. The workers drank strong beer because they thought it made them stronger. Because Franklin drank water, he was called the "Water-American."[10] Yet Franklin could carry more trays of heavy type up and down stairs than they could.

Soon Franklin was asked to change from working with the presses to making up the type. The new group of men Franklin worked with expected him to pay into the kitty for drinks. Franklin declined because he had already paid into the kitty of the group working the presses. So the others played many tricks on his work, mixing up what he had put together but saying that it was a ghost that did the damage. Finally, in order to get along with the others, Franklin gave in and paid.

Franklin worked hard and was well-liked. He did not take Monday off the way others sometimes did. He could work fast. As a result, he was well paid and found it easier to save money.

Franklin taught John Wygate, one of his friends from work, how to swim. He could do tricks on and under the water that others found fun. Indeed one father offered to pay Franklin to teach his two sons how to swim. However, by the time he had this offer, he had already decided to return to America.

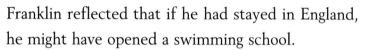

Sayings of Benjamin Franklin

"There are no gains without pains."

"Eat to live—not live to eat."

"If you would be loved, love and be lovable."

"He that cannot obey, cannot command."

"Never leave that till tomorrow which you can do today."

"Early to bed and early to rise, Makes a man healthy, wealthy, and wise."[11]

Franklin reflected that if he had stayed in England, he might have opened a swimming school.

Wygate was not only a swimming companion but also enjoyed reading about the same kinds of subjects that Franklin did. Wygate proposed that the two of them travel around Europe, working along the way at print shops. Franklin liked the idea.

Franklin talked to his old friend, Thomas Denham, about the matter. Denham thought that it was time for Franklin to return to Pennsylvania. He offered him a job as a clerk and bookkeeper in his store in Philadelphia. Later he would send Franklin on buying trips on which he could make money. Though the starting pay was less than Franklin was getting from printing, the prospect for making more money in the future was better. Franklin was getting tired of London anyway, and he wanted to return to America.

Besides, Franklin had great respect for Denham. He was becoming wiser about his choice of friends. Denham, who had failed in business in England, went to America, where he made his fortune. When he returned to England, he invited the people to whom he owed money to dinner. Denham thanked these people for their patience. They had not expected to be repaid. When the dinner plates were removed, each of them found on the table their payment in full with interest on the debt.

Franklin had lived in London for eighteen months. He had worked hard and spent little on himself except for plays and books. His friend, Ralph, borrowed money from Franklin that amounted to twenty-seven pounds—more than half the fifty pounds that Franklin was supposed to earn in a year from Denham in 1726. Franklin had no hope of being repaid this amount. Although Franklin was not able to save much in London, he had learned a lot and made many friends.

He sailed from England on July 23, 1726. On the trip home, Franklin made a plan for his life that he adhered to pretty much until old age. He was glad that he had made a life plan when he was so young so that he could regulate his future conduct.

Unfortunately, this plan was not found in the journal that he kept.

What was Franklin to discover on his return to Philadelphia? What would the governor say to him? Would Deborah Read still be his friend? How would the deal with Denham work out?

4

Settling Down

Though Franklin sailed from England on July 23, 1726, it took until October 11 before he landed in Philadelphia. He learned that Sir William Keith was no longer the governor. When he saw Keith walking along the street, he thought that the man looked a little embarassed. Keith said nothing—he offered no excuses for sending Franklin off to England without the promised funding.

Franklin admitted that he should have felt ashamed when he met Deborah Read. After all, he had written her only one letter, though they had wanted to marry before he left.[1] Her friends had persuaded her to give up hope of his return and to marry someone else. She had married John Rogers, who was a good potter but a poor husband. Deborah was not happy with him. When she learned that he had another wife, she left him and refused to use his name. Rogers borrowed a great deal of money and ran away to the West Indies.

Getting to Work in Philadelphia

Thomas Denham, for whom Franklin now worked, opened his store. They sold the things that they had brought from England. Franklin studied the shop and became an expert salesman. Denham was like a father to Franklin, giving him advice and caring about him. He lent Franklin money over and above his wages. Unfortunately, just after Franklin turned twenty-one both he and Denham fell ill. Denham died, and Franklin nearly did. Franklin had pleurisy, inflamed lung tissue. When he wrote his autobiography, Franklin could not recall what Denham died of—only that his friend had a long illness.

In his will, Denham forgave Franklin's debt. However, after Denham died, the store was taken over by the people who handled Denham's property. Franklin was out of work again. His brother-in-law, Holmes, who now also lived in Philadelphia, advised him to return to printing.

Though Franklin's old boss, Keimer, had improved his print shop and now sold paper as well, he had a number of workers who were not very skilled or experienced. However, business was good, because there were still only two print shops in the city.

Keimer offered Franklin a job managing the print shop. In London, Franklin had heard bad things about Keimer, so he did not want to have anything more to do with him.[2] But Franklin could not find other work, so he took the job. He was paid good wages in order to teach the lower-paid workers how to do the job. He thought it likely that after the others knew how to do things, he would be let go.

Franklin had to teach a mixed group of men. One was an Oxford University student who got into debt and came to America under contract to work for four years. Others were right off the farm with little schooling.

Sometimes Franklin had to create molds for type the shop did not have. He could engrave (a process of cutting into metal or wood) letters or a picture that would then be used in printing. He made the ink and kept track of the stores of paper.

As the other workers became skilled, Keimer told Franklin that he thought he was paying him too much money. Franklin tried to put up with him in order to keep his job. One day Franklin heard a loud noise outside near the courthouse. He stuck his head out of the window to see what it was. His boss

Franklin's Words on Aging

"At twenty years of age, the will reigns; at thirty, the wit; and at forty, the judgment." (June 1741)[3]

in the street below told him to get back to work. With all the people listening, the boss reprimanded Franklin. He then came up into the shop and continued his scolding. Franklin quit on the spot.

Starting New Projects

Hugh Meredith, one of the other workers, brought some of Franklin's things from work over to his home that evening. He talked Franklin out of moving, and suggested that they go into business together in the spring, when his contract with their boss was up. Meredith thought that his father would support this endeavor. With Franklin's skill and Meredith's father's money, they could be partners. Franklin met with Meredith's father and gave him a list of things that would be needed for a print shop.

While waiting to begin the new business, Franklin could not find work at the other printer's shop. His old boss, however, received an order from New Jersey to make some paper money and needed Franklin's help. So the two made up, and Franklin went back to work. Franklin made a copper plate press for the job—the first in America.

At last, in 1726, Franklin was able to set up his own shop with some friends. Another friend, George House, sent them their first customer just after they opened. It was a small print job bringing in only five shillings. Since they had spent all their money on supplies, they needed the cash. Franklin said that this first sum they earned gave him more happiness than much larger amounts they made later. Ever after, Franklin always liked to help young people just starting out.

About this time, Franklin formed a club with his friends. They called it the Junto. The club met on Friday evenings, and members were required to come with one or two questions on serious subjects. Every three months, members had to write an essay on any subject. One person was to moderate the discussion. The goal was not to win a debate but to try to understand the subject. The club lasted about forty years. It provided good experience in reading, writing, and speaking.

Franklin's shop did well. Some had thought the town could not support three printers, and that Franklin would fail, but he worked very hard and did good work. One important man said of Franklin: "For the industry of that Franklin is superior to anything I ever saw of the kind; I see him still at work

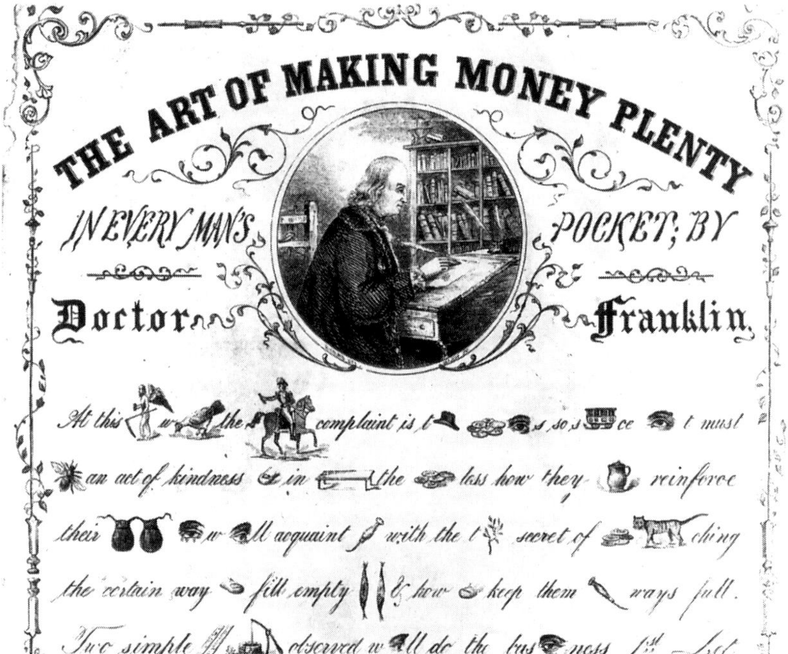

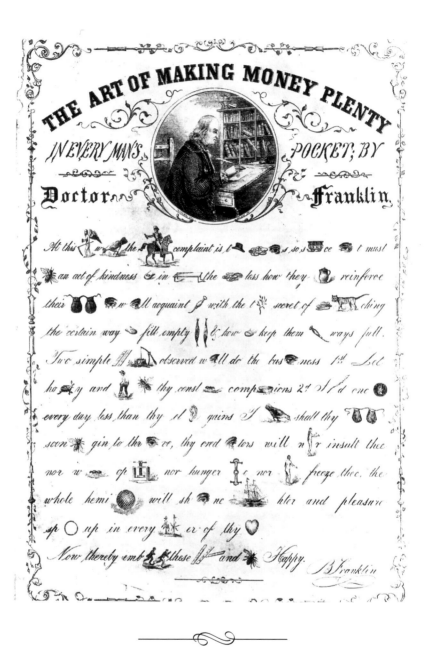

Franklin was successful in business and saving. Here he gives his secrets to his readers in the form of a puzzle.

when I go home from the club, and he is at work again before his neighbors are out of bed."[4]

Franklin began publishing a newspaper. He did so by playing the two rival printers against each other. At the time, the only newspaper in Philadelphia, the *American Weekly Mercury,* was put out by Bradford. It was poorly managed, not entertaining, but profitable. When Keimer put out a new paper, *The Universal Instructor in All Arts and Sciences: and Pennsylvania Gazette,* that promised to succeed, Franklin wrote some pieces for Bradford that helped the *Mercury* and hurt the *Gazette.* When Keimer's newspaper failed, Franklin bought it in 1729 and renamed it *The Pennsylvania Gazette*. It turned a good profit in a few years.

Meredith, his partner, did not do much work. He did not have much skill and was drunk most of the time.[5] Meredith's father, who was supposed to have paid for their presses and supplies, could not afford to do so. Finally Meredith decided he was in the wrong trade. He sold his share to Franklin, moved to North Carolina, and bought a farm. Two of Franklin's friends lent him money to pay off the debts of the shop. By 1729, Franklin was in business by himself.

Franklin made sure that people saw that he was a hard worker. He did not spend money on fancy clothes, but instead dressed plainly. He was not above manual labor and even pushed a wheelbarrow full of paper he bought for his shop. As his business grew, he hired others to help him with the new work that came to him.

Keimer sold his print shop and moved to the West Indies. The buyer was not a hard worker, did not do well, and soon left town, taking the presses with him. That left the city with just two printers.

Finding a Wife

Franklin rented part of his home to a family who had a daughter. Her parents thought Franklin might be a good match for her. But when Franklin asked for money to get out of debt if he married her, the parents backed off and would not let him date the girl. They moved out of Franklin's house.

According to Franklin, this made him think more about getting married. A more likely reason is that Franklin had fathered a son, named William, out of wedlock. Who the mother of the child was, no one has been able to discover.[6] Some said it was a servant in his house. Others think it may have been Deborah Read. In any event, the scandal would be less if Franklin kept the name of his son's mother secret. That is what he did, though it did not stop speculation as he became more involved in public life.

Deborah Read moved in as Franklin's common-law wife on September 1, 1730. A common-law marriage is when two people agree that they are married, even if they do not have a marriage certificate. Franklin was then twenty-four years old, and Deborah was twenty-five. Since it was not easy to prove that her legal husband, Rogers, was dead or had another wife, a wedding in church was out of the question. Also, if Franklin had officially married Deborah, he might have been charged with the debts that Rogers had left her.

The match between Deborah and Benjamin Franklin was a good one. She moved in with him in the house that was also his shop. She helped look after the shop and folded and stitched papers. She brought up William. They later had another son, Francis, and a daughter, Sarah.

Deborah was willing to adopt the simple lifestyle that her husband had chosen. They had no servants and ate inexpensively. But one day, Deborah bought Franklin a better bowl and a silver spoon. That was the first of what would amount to a good set of china they eventually acquired.

Planning for Life

During this time, Franklin began several projects to benefit the city. With some other young men, he donated money to start the first library. Franklin was pleased that strangers noted that the people of his city were more literate than those of many other countries.

Benjamin Franklin made his money through his print shop, newspaper, and books. The citizens of Philadelphia recognized him as an up-and-coming businessman.

Franklin also thought a lot about his own life. He wanted to be perfect.[7] Although he supported the Presbyterian Church, he rarely attended services. Instead, he made up a prayer service for himself. He also had a list of thirteen virtues that he wanted in his life.

Each week he picked one from the list to work on. Each day, he kept a record of instances in which he did not do what he thought he should. He felt that he could make himself follow good habits this way.[8] It was tougher than he expected, but he kept at it.[9] He even made up a little book on ivory so that he could keep his daily score card and wipe out his marks with a wet sponge. He carried the book with him on trips.

As part of his goal to set things in order, he set a schedule for himself. He was to get up at five o'clock in the morning to wash and pray. Each morning he was to ask himself, "What good shall I do this day?"[10] He studied and ate breakfast. At eight o'clock, he was at work. At noon, he broke for reading, checking his accounts, and eating lunch. He went back to work from two until six o'clock. Then he was to put things back in their places, have supper, and have music or conversation. At the end of the day, he was to ask: "What good have I done to-day?"[11] Then he slept from ten o'clock at night until five o'clock the next morning.

Thirteen virtues Franklin tried to practice

1. Temperance [not eating or drinking too much]
2. Silence [speaking what matters]
3. Order [having things in place, time used well]
4. Resolution [doing what you are supposed to do]
5. Frugality [spending only to do good, wasting nothing]
6. Industry [always doing something useful, losing no time]
7. Sincerity [not hurting others by lying, being just]
8. Justice [not wronging others or forgetting benefits you owe others]
9. Moderation [avoiding extremes]
10. Cleanliness [keeping body, clothes, and house clean]
11. Tranquillity [not being upset by small things or things that cannot be helped]
12. Chastity [keeping sex under control]
13. Humility [avoiding pride][12]

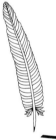

Becoming a Business and Civic Leader

In 1732, he first published his almanac—a calendar of weather forecasts and sayings. Franklin liked to write under the name of imaginary characters and used the name Richard Saunders for this book—probably after the name of an English author. So it became known as *Poor Richard's Almanac*. James Franklin was publishing a *Poor Robin* almanac in

Newport. Benjamin Franklin tried to fill all the space on the pages of his almanac in order to educate the people who bought the book—often the only book they bought.

Franklin also viewed his newspaper as a way of teaching people. He refused to print items he knew were not true or would hurt others. He did not think much of papers that did so.

Some of his ideas about education were unconventional in his time. He felt a woman would benefit more from knowing how to keep business accounts than being taught music or dancing. Franklin told of a widow who had been raised in Holland who sent him better business reports than her husband had.[13] Also, he thought that it was better to learn French, Italian, or Spanish before Latin because it was easier to do so and more useful.[14]

After ten years of being away from Boston, he made a trip home. On his way home, he stopped at Newport to see his brother, James. This time, he made peace with him. James was ill and asked his brother to look after his ten-year-old son after he died. Franklin did so, sending the boy to school and taking him into his shop. Franklin did this as a way to make up for leaving James's shop before his contract was up.

One of Franklin's greatest losses was the death

Poor Richard, 1733.

AN

Almanack

For the Year of Chriſt

1733,

Being the Firſt after LEAP YEAR:

And makes ſince the Creation	Years
By the Account of the Eastern *Greeks*	7241
By the Latin Church, when ☉ ent. ♈	6932
By the Computation of *W. W.*	5742
By the *Roman* Chronology	5682
By the *Jewish* Rabbies	5494

Wherein is contained

The Lunations, Eclipſes, Judgment of the Weather, Spring Tides, Planets Motions & mutual Aſpects, Sun and Moon's Riſing and Setting, Length of Days, Time of High Water, Fairs, Courts, and obſervable Days.

Fitted to the Latitude of Forty Degrees, and a Meridian of Five Hours Weſt from *London*, but may without ſenſible Error, ſerve all the adjacent Places, even from *Newfoundland* to *South-Carolina*.

By *RICHARD SAUNDERS*, Philom.

PHILADELPHIA:
Printed and ſold by *B. FRANKLIN*, at the New Printing-Office near the Market.

Franklin's Poor Richard's Almanac *(spelled Almanack back then) was a best-seller. He wrote under the name of Richard Saunders. The book contained weather predictions and hints for good living.*

of his four-year-old son, Francis, in 1736. The boy died of smallpox. Franklin regretted that he had not had his son inoculated—injected with a vaccine to prevent the disease. This new treatment was just beginning to be used. Franklin was in favor of it but was waiting for Francis to recover from an illness before having him inoculated.

Franklin entered public office in 1736. He was elected clerk of the legislature in 1736 and appointed postmaster in 1737. Franklin had many ideas which greatly improved the city of Philadelphia. He came up with the idea of a tax to provide better watchmen. Franklin also helped form groups of volunteer firefighters. With the purchase of fire engines, hooks, and ladders, he helped Philadelphia cut down huge losses caused by fire. He supported a famous preacher, George Whitfield, in building an orphanage to care for children with no parents. Franklin also had ideas for a college, a group to support adult study, and a voluntary group of fighters for the city's defense. He thought of having a lottery to pay for cannons to be set up to defend the city. In order to do his part to defend the city, he also took his turn as a common soldier.

His printing and newspaper business had grown. He had set up partners in other colonies who were successful. Franklin reached the point where he could retire early and do what he liked

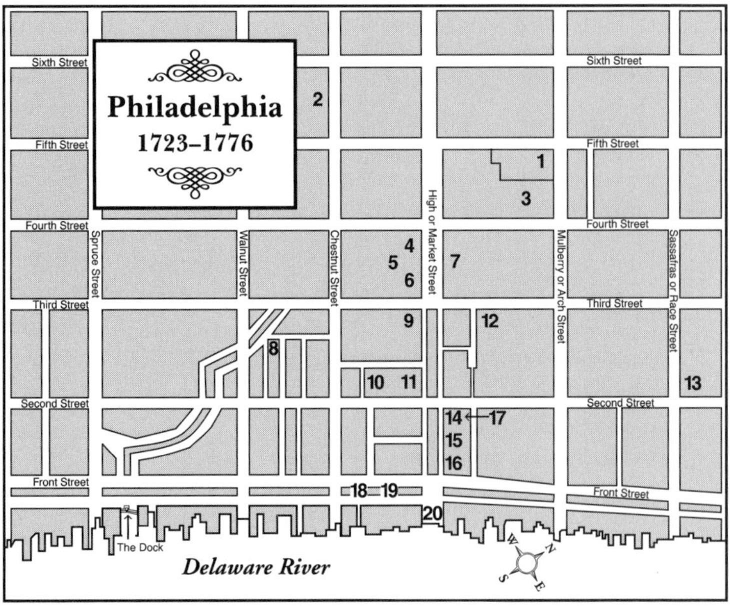

This map of the streets of Philadelphia shows some of the places that were important in Benjamin Franklin's life.

1. Graves of Francis Folger Franklin, 1763, and Deborah Franklin, 1774, in Christ Church Burying Ground.
2. State House (Independence Hall), occupied 1735.
3. "New Building," erected 1740; acquired for Academy and College.
4. Franklin's residence, 326 Market St., 1761–1765.
5. Franklin's house, completed 1765.
6. John Read's residence; Samuel Keimer's printing office was next door, 1723–1726.
7. Franklin's residence, 325 Market St., 1751–1761; Post Office, 1752–1753.
8. Masonic Lodge, erected 1755.
9. Indian King Tavern, a meeting place for Junto and Masonic Lodge.
10. Probable site of Samuel Keimer's printing office, 1726–1730.
11. Friends' Meeting Houses: Great Meeting House, 1696–1755; Greater Meeting House, 1755–1804.
12. William Franklin's Post Office, 1753–1757.
13. Franklin's residence, 1748–1750.
14. Franklin's residence, 141 Market St., 1750–1751.
15. Franklin's residence, 139 Market St., 1728–1739.
16. Franklin's residence 131 Market St., 1739–1748; printing office, 1739–1752.
17. Site of early meetings of Library Company.
18. Thomas Denham's shop, where Franklin was clerk, 1726–1727.
19. Crooked Billet Tavern, where Franklin spent his first night, 1723.
20. Market Street Wharf, where Franklin landed, 1723.

the most—study and invent. In 1742, he improved the method of heating rooms with his invention of a type of stove. A version of it is still called the Franklin stove. By 1748, when he was forty-two years old, he had the time and money to do what he wanted. He wanted to learn more about electricity.

5

Retiring Early to New Careers

Electricity is what made Franklin's name known in Europe as well as America. Franklin had been curious about this subject since a visit to Boston a few years before his retirement. There he met Dr. Archibald Spence, who had arrived recently from Scotland and had given a demonstration of electricity. The next year Spence gave another demonstration in Philadelphia. In those days very little was known about electricity. Franklin came up with theories about what electricity was and ways to test his ideas.

People back then knew that they could shuffle their feet on a rug and get a mild shock if they touched something else. Scientists had developed a friction machine that made an electrical charge. The first Leyden jar (also called a Leyden bottle) was invented in 1746. This glass jar was coated with tin foil and had a metallic rod passing through the lid that contacted the inner lining, condensing static electricity. William Watson of London said that all bodies have electricity.

Experimenting with Electricity

Franklin was curious about these new ideas. Peter Collinson of London sent Franklin and his friends a glass tube and data about how to use it for experiments. Some early scientists charged glass tubes with electricity by rubbing them with silk. Franklin experimented with this tube. He reported, "My house was continually full, for some time, with people who came to see these new wonders."[1] Franklin had more glass tubes made. He wrote out two lectures for a neighbor to use to demonstrate for the people these new ideas. That neighbor took his show on the road through the colonies and made some money from the project.

Franklin wrote back to Collinson telling him of his success in using the tube. Collinson thought the letters should be read at the Royal Society in London, an important group of scientists. They laughed at Franklin's paper. Still, some of his friends thought his letters were of value and had them printed up in a pamphlet. It was in France that his ideas about electricity had the greatest impact, when Count de Buffon had them translated into French. Later his book was to be printed in Italian and German.

What made people take notice of Franklin's ideas was that he had said you could draw lightning from the clouds. At first this was done with a pointed rod. In France, the "Philadelphia experiments" were done for the king and his court. Large crowds gathered in Paris to see them. These pointed rods were eventually made into lightning rods to protect buildings that were struck. The rod channeled the electricity into a safe route to the ground, thereby preventing fires.

Some of Franklin's experiments were extremely dangerous. He decided to try to kill his Christmas turkey by giving it an electric shock. By accident, he made contact with the current. There was a bright flash of light. A sound like the crack of a pistol followed. Franklin was knocked senseless, his body shaking violently. Gradually, he came to. He made a joke of it, saying that he was as bad as the man who, in order to steal gun powder, made a hole in the barrel with a hot iron.[2]

In 1752, Franklin also tried to show that lightning was electricity by flying a kite on a stormy day. No written account by Franklin of this attempt has survived, although he was interviewed by a famous English scientist, Joseph Priestley.

Priestley told the story fifteen years later. Franklin's twenty-one-year-old son, William, helped him with the kite. The kite had a sharp pointed wire at the top. At the end of the kite string, he tied a silk ribbon to which a key was fastened. The lightning struck the kite, and electricity flowed down to the key. Franklin had to wait out a number of clouds to succeed.[3] Again, Franklin was not aware of how dangerous this was. He proved that lightning was electricity, but luckily he did not get a strong enough charge to hurt him. The following year, a Swedish physicist trying to put up an experimental rod was killed.

Franklin is famous for his experiments with electricity.

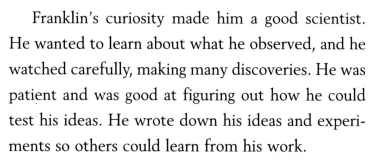

Words First Used by Franklin

Franklin was the first to use many electrical terms still current today: "armature, battery, brush, charged, charging, condense, conductor, discharge, electrical fire, electrical shock, electrician, electrified, electrify, electrized, Leyden bottle, minus [negative or negatively], negatively, non-conducting, non-conductor, non-electric, plus [positive or positively], stroke [electric shock], uncharged."[4]

Franklin's curiosity made him a good scientist. He wanted to learn about what he observed, and he watched carefully, making many discoveries. He was patient and was good at figuring out how he could test his ideas. He wrote down his ideas and experiments so others could learn from his work.

People in Europe were surprised that an American so far from other scientists had made these discoveries. Besides, Franklin was a tradesman—not a teacher. He did not have the schooling that most scientists had.[5]

In the six years from the summer of 1746 when Franklin began his experiments to 1752 when he flew his kite, he had turned electricity from a mere curiosity into something to be studied scientifically. He was given honorary degrees by Harvard College,

Yale College, and the College of William and Mary. The Royal Society in London gave him a gold medal in 1753 and made him a member in 1756. While pleased with this medal, Franklin was modest about it. He did not patent the lightning rod or try to profit from it.

While electricity made him famous, Franklin was also interested in other sciences. He was one of the first to study the weather and suggested how air might move to produce storms. Rock formations and fossils of seashells interested him, too. Franklin studied medicines and made a medical device (a catheter, a tube inserted in a body cavity to withdraw liquid) for his sick brother. He talked with others about how the pores of the skin worked and how blood circulated. He wondered if ants had some way of talking with each other. Franklin had theories about how to raise pigeons. He experimented with planting crops and urged that land should not be wasted. Farming and gardening were to be taught in the academy school he was planning. He was also curious about air and light.

Concerning Himself with Government

Not all of Franklin's time was spent on science, however. A Congress made up of members from the colonies was called to consider means of defense against the French and their Native American allies. They had been harassing and killing settlers in the

Franklin's experiments with electricity made him famous in America and Europe. Often his pictures include a lightning strike as a reminder of his work.

western regions of the colonies. Governor James Hamilton of Pennsylvania chose Franklin to be one of the representatives of his colony. Franklin drew up a plan for all the colonies to unite under one government. The president was to be chosen by the British king. However, the legislatures of the colonies were to select members of a Council. Franklin's plan was sent to England and the colonies. England thought it gave too much power to the colonies. The colonists thought that England was given too much power. The plan was not approved.

The various colonies had different forms of government. Some were under the direct control of the king. For others, like Pennsylvania, the king had granted the land to his supporters. William Penn had been given the land that became Pennsylvania in 1681. He used it as a place where the Quakers and others might practice their religion in freedom. When Penn died, his heirs, who were not Quakers, took over the land and leased it. They wanted to make money from Pennsylvania. The people who settled on this land thought that Penn's heirs should help pay for protection against hostile Native Americans.

Franklin became an important member of the Pennsylvania legislature. He was asked to be part of the group that made a treaty with the Native Americans. There he saw firsthand how drinking

William Penn (standing with arms open) founded Pennsylvania. He was a Quaker but allowed people of all religions to settle there. Here, he negotiates a treaty in 1681 with the local Native Americans.

rum had helped to make the Native Americans lose their land. The Native Americans were not given any rum while the treaty was being made. Afterward, they were given the rum they wanted. The Native Americans built a big bonfire and chased each other with burning sticks. This fire, the fighting, and the "horrid yellings" made Franklin think of hell.[6]

From 1754 to 1763, the French with their Native American allies attacked the British in the American colonies. The Native Americans attacked the colonists who settled on the frontier where land was available. Whole families of settlers were killed. To make matters worse, the Native Americans were receiving aid and advice from the French, who did not like the English. Something had to be done.

The British sent over troops of their regular army to help fight the French and Indian War. The British soldiers were used to fighting European style in ordered lines instead of using the trees and landscape for cover. They expected to find supplies from the farms along the way. They did not know how to fend for themselves where there were no farms.

Advising on the Defense of the Frontier

In 1755, when Franklin was forty-nine, he and his son, William, went to Frederick, Maryland, to meet the British General Edward Braddock. In Maryland, the general could obtain only twenty-five of the one hundred fifty wagons with horses needed to carry his supplies. Franklin told the general that in Pennsylvania almost every farmer had a wagon. Rather than have the British commandeer the wagons, Franklin, in his own name, contracted with the farmers. He hired the wagons for a sum of money that he expected the British would pay.

Also, Franklin tried to suggest to the general that the march and the fighting would not be as easy as the British expected. He told General Braddock about the fighting tactics the Native Americans used, such as ambushes, surprise attacks on the flanks, and the cutting off of supply lines. Still the general marched his troops through forests, a long way from the supply base. When the army was bunched in an open place after crossing a river just short of Fort Duquesne (now Pittsburgh), the Native Americans attacked. First, they picked off the officers who were on horses. About two thirds of the troops were killed. The rest of the troops took horses from the wagons and fled. They left their guns and supplies behind. General Braddock was wounded and was carried off the field. Four hundred Native Americans and French had killed or wounded 63 of the 86 British officers and killed 714 of the 1100 soldiers. The British retreated all the way to Philadelphia.

Franklin noted that this defeat "gave us Americans the first suspicion that our exalted ideas of the prowess of the British regulars had not been well founded."[7] Franklin was highly praised by General Braddock in his reports to London. Perhaps because the British were defeated, Franklin received no benefit from his efforts.

So how could the settlers on the frontier be protected? The colonists agreed to pay a tax for defense. They also looked to the English owners of Pennsylvania for help and were given some money.

The British General Braddock was wounded in a battle against the French and Native Americans. Franklin supplied wagons to the general for his fight.

Franklin was put in charge of spending this money. The governor asked Franklin to take over the defense of the northwestern frontier, which was enemy land. Franklin was to raise troops and build a string of forts. He had no training for this work. With the help of his son, William, who had been an officer in the war against the French in Canada, he took on the job.

Franklin had written a law to support a volunteer army. He brought some of these troops together at Bethlehem, Pennsylvania. This town had been settled by the Moravians, a group of people from eastern Europe. Previously, the Native Americans had burned another village settled by the Moravians and had killed all the people. When Franklin marched to that village, he first had to bury the dead in better graves. Then, he and his troops set about building a wooden fort.

Always the scientist, Franklin made observations even out at the frontier. On his watch, he timed how fast two men cut down a fourteen-inch-thick pine tree. They accomplished this task in six minutes. He also noted that the Native Americans had a good system of keeping their feet warm while spying on the fort. They dug holes in the ground where they placed charcoal fires so that no light or smoke escaped to warn of their presence. Franklin looked at the way the Moravians let smoke out of their buildings by placing holes at regular spaces just under the ceiling. He also marveled at the way the Moravian elders arranged marriages for their young people—using a lottery system if there was not an obvious match.

In a week, in spite of rain, Franklin's men had finished building. He was not sure that the structure they built could really be called a fort since the walls were not very strong. However, since the Native Americans did not have any cannons, it was sufficient.

Franklin roughed it along with his men. He slept

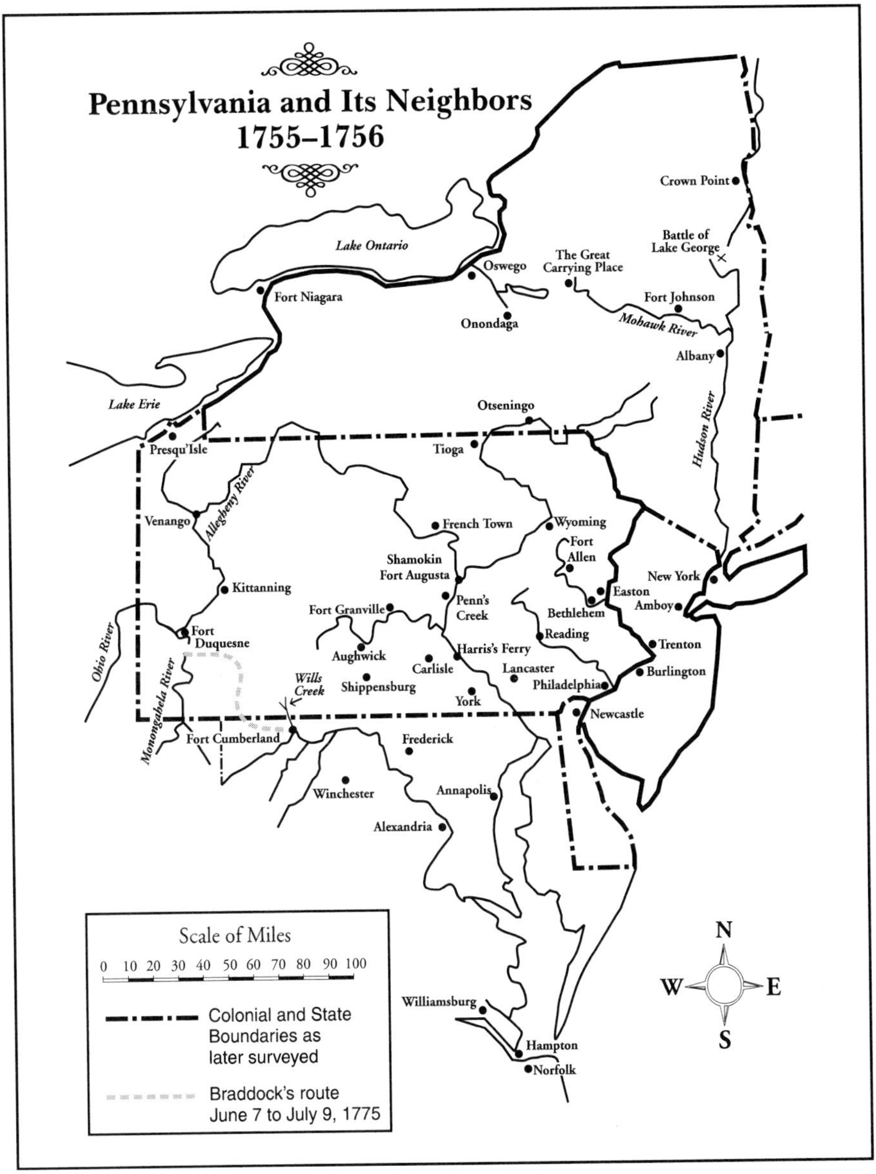

This map shows some of the places Franklin visited during the French and Indian War. At that time, he was advising the British on how to protect the frontier.

on the wooden floor, wrapped only in a blanket or two. Shortly, however, he was needed back in Philadelphia. He found Colonel William Clapham, an officer who had fought Native Americans before, to take over his command.

Back home, the officers of his volunteer army chose Franklin to be colonel of their troops. He had about one thousand two hundred well-armed men. The men liked Franklin. They gave him a mounted escort when he had to leave on a trip to Virginia. When news of this escort reached London, Franklin was told that this parade was only for princes. In any event, the law in England that made officers in the colonies was overturned, so he was not a colonel for long.

Going to London to Represent Pennsylvania

The legislature, upset with the actions of the heirs of William Penn (the man who was granted Pennsylvania by the king), decided to send Franklin to London to reason with them. So, in 1757, Franklin set out on the long sea trip to England. The ship was almost lost on the rocks as she neared the coast of Great Britain. Only a lighthouse and the quick action of a passenger, Captain Kennedy, saved her. The ship's captain was asleep, but Kennedy, a Naval captain, saw the danger and ordered a change of course just in time. Franklin decided that he would encourage the building of more lighthouses in America if he lived to return there.[8]

When Franklin reached London, he found that the British had a different opinion about the rights of Americans. Many of the British argued that whatever the king said was law. Franklin did not agree. He said that the king had given Americans certain rights when he made a contract with Penn.

Franklin did not find it easy to deal with Penn's heirs, who governed under the charter from the king. They feared that the Americans would drain off their money with demands for help. Penn's heirs delayed, but Franklin kept after them. At last, they sent an answer—not directly to Franklin—but to their governor. The legislature in Pennsylvania did not even bother to discuss the answer.

Still, Franklin's stay in London was pleasant in other ways. He had come over with his son, who was to study law there. Also, he brought two servants from Philadelphia. Franklin bought cloth, shoes, wigs, and swords so that he was well dressed. He settled into four rooms in the home of Margaret Stevenson, a widow, who lived with her daughter Mary.

Franklin was like a father to Mary. He hoped his son would marry her, but this never happened. Franklin also took an interest in Mary's education.

He once wrote to her: "I would advise you to read with a pen in your hand, and enter in a little book short hints of what you find that is curious, or that may be useful . . ."[9] He taught her a great deal about science. Since there were words she might not know, he advised: ". . . I think it would be well for you to have a good dictionary at hand, to consult immediately when you meet with a word you do not comprehend the precise meaning of."[10] He knew that at first looking up words would seem like trouble.[11] However, as she learned more words, she would find science easier to learn and more fun since she would understand more.

With Mrs. Stevenson's help, he purchased several boxes of clothing, china, silver, carpets, and other goods to send home to his wife and daughter. Now he had the money and the position to merit these luxuries. He kept some of the silver and china to use in his rooms in London.

Franklin had a circle of friends he enjoyed. He made more friends in England and especially Scotland. In 1759, he was given honorary degrees from St. Andrews University in Scotland, and later in 1762 from Oxford University in England. He emphasized to the British the value of America to them. He found that they knew very little about the colonies.

Nothing gave Franklin more pleasure during his

time in England than his invention of a musical instrument.[12] He put thirty-seven specially blown glasses of different sizes on an iron rod. The rod went through the center of the glasses. They were arranged so that each was inside but not touching the next largest size. The player sat in front of the instrument and turned the rod with a foot on a treadle (a lever or pedal moved by the foot) like a

Franklin continued his writing and editing when he was in England. He increased his number of friends abroad and was given honors there.

spinning wheel. The player made music by touching the edges of the moving glasses with his or her fingers. Franklin called it an armonica. It was in fashion for many years. Franklin also learned how to play the harp, guitar, and violin.

Returning to Public Service in America

At last in January 1762, Franklin decided to go back home to America since there was little more that he could accomplish in Britain. Because Britain and France were still at war on the seas, his ship had to go in a convoy of other boats for safety. When he reached Philadelphia, his friends came to his house to greet him. They told him that if they had known he was coming, they would have met him with five hundred horses. While away in Britain, he had been elected to the Pennsylvania legislature as a sign of respect for him and his mission.

Before the convoy sailed, Franklin's son, William, had been appointed governor of New Jersey. Perhaps the British did this to try to influence Franklin to side with them. If so, they were mistaken.

Franklin missed his friends in London.[13] He continued to write to Mary Stevenson. He even thought of moving to England if he could talk his wife into the trip across the ocean.

Franklin had enemies at home who accused him of living too richly abroad. Franklin countered this rumor by making an accounting to the legislature in which he charged only about half the sum that had been allotted for him to spend in England. The members allowed him to keep the full amount and voted to give him more for his five-year service to them. They realized the value of Franklin's work in Britain.

During his first year home, Franklin spent a great deal of time on his work as head of the post office. In his role as Deputy Postmaster General of North America, he visited post offices from Virginia to New England. The British occupied Canada at the time, so he arranged for mail service from New York to Montreal and Quebec. Also for the first time, mail traveled by both night and day between Philadelphia, New York, and Boston.

In 1763, the British and French signed a peace treaty. Peace did not extend to the Native Americans. They attacked the English from Detroit, Michigan, to Fort Pitt, at Pittsburgh, Pennsylvania. They killed families living along the frontier. Some of the settlers reacted by rioting and killing even friendly Native Americans. Near Bethlehem, the Moravians took in some friendly Native Americans to try to protect them from rioters and moved them to Philadelphia.

Tension was high in Philadelphia. Franklin argued

for protection for the Native Americans though it made him enemies. He wrote,

> If an Indian injures me, does it follow that I may revenge that injury on all Indians? . . . If it be right to kill men for such a reason, then, should any man with a freckled face and red hair kill a wife or child of mine, it would be right for me to revenge it by killing all the freckled red-haired men, women, and children I could afterwards anywhere meet with.[14]

When the rioters approached Philadelphia, the governor ran to Franklin's house at midnight for advice. Franklin and other citizens armed themselves in preparation. The rioters found the city defended. Franklin went out to meet with the rioters. Faced with the show of force and swayed by Franklin's reasoning, the rioters turned back.

This event brought to a head the conflict between Franklin and the Penns. The grandson of William Penn offered money for Native American scalps—those of men or women. Franklin said that the Pennsylvania legislature had lost all respect for the way Penn had dealt with the rioters. The Penns labeled Franklin a villain for causing discontent.

Franklin was elected to be speaker of the legislature, the one who presided over the meetings. In this office, he signed a petition asking the king to take over the government of Pennsylvania. Such an action would remove the Penns from control of the colony. In the next election, one party supported the Penns. Franklin did not and was voted out of office. However, his party still controlled the legislature. They voted to send the petition to the king and made Franklin their messenger. Franklin quickly left for London. He left behind his wife and daughter because Deborah Franklin did not want to cross the ocean. He also had to leave the new house he was building.

Defending the Colonies in London

Franklin had a tough job ahead in London. The Pennsylvania legislature wanted him to ask for change, but he was not to make any agreements that would cost people their liberty. For example, the proposed Stamp Act required the people to buy stamps to put on legal documents, newspapers, stationery, almanacs, and even dice and playing cards. Representing the colonies, Franklin opposed that idea. Franklin wanted to see the British Empire hold together and be friendly to the American colonies. He expected to be away only a few months, but he stayed ten years.

In Britain, he settled in once again with the Stevensons. Also, he found old friends and made new ones with whom to carry on his other interests. He did not have much time for recreation though, because politics kept him busy. The British king, George III, said that he could not interfere with the Penns. King George did not want to give the Americans any

George III became the king of England in 1760. At first, Franklin thought that he would be a good king, but he found him and his advisors hard to deal with.

opportunity to spell out what they wanted. They were being vocal enough about the Stamp Act.

In 1765, the Stamp Act passed in England in spite of Franklin's efforts to kill it. The American colonists protested more violently than Franklin had expected. Patrick Henry in Virginia blasted the act. Groups joined together in the colonies, taking the name "Sons of Liberty." The colonists had no representatives in the British legislature that passed the Stamp Act. "No taxation without representation" became the slogan of the Americans. They ignored the Stamp Act and stopped buying British goods.

Franklin's political enemies at home said that Franklin had written the Stamp Act and that he had been paid to provide names of colonial officers to enforce it. Some threatened to burn down Franklin's new house. William Franklin came over from New Jersey to bring Deborah Franklin and his sister back with him. Deborah sent her daughter with William, but she stayed to defend the house with the help of others. She thought she would have more friends than enemies if anyone gave her trouble.[15]

Contrary to what his opponents claimed, Franklin was hard at work to get the Stamp Act overturned. He enlisted support from the British merchants who were hurt by the act because of loss of sales to the colonies. He wrote letters to the newspapers, and he was even ordered to appear before the British legislature. He was known by most of the members and represented the colonies well.

Franklin talked about how the colonists had helped the British in their fight against the Native Americans and the French. This was clever because the British thought of themselves as helping the American colonists. He emphasized and explained how the act was hurting British trade. Before the act, colonists liked to buy the fashions and goods of Great Britain. Franklin said that after the act, the colonists would "wear their old clothes over again till they can make new ones."[16] The act was overturned in March 1766—thanks, in part, to Franklin's efforts.

Back in Philadelphia, Ben Franklin was a hero. With no stamp tax, people there promised to wear suits made in Britain on the king's birthday. Now that there was no boycott against buying British goods, Franklin sent his wife some fancy British cloth for a dress. However, Franklin was uneasy about British attitudes. He could see that the Americans would not be allowed to vote in the British legislature. Even if the British ever offered representation in the government, he feared the Americans would no longer be willing to accept it because of the way they had been treated.

Franklin had some financial worries, too. His printing partnership back in Pennsylvania was about to end because Franklin had political differences with his partner. If he lost his post office job because of his efforts in London, he would not have as much income as he had in the past. He wrote his wife to cut back spending except for purchases needed for their daughter, who was about to be married. If the young couple required more, they would just have to work for it as Franklin and his wife had.

As it turned out, he kept his post office job. He was also asked to be a representative in London not only for Pennsylvania but also for Georgia, New Jersey, and Massachusetts. He had plenty of work ahead of him. Britain was continually trying to think up new ways to get money from the colonies. Franklin felt that the colonies should be part of the British Empire but with American members voting in the British legislature. He could see that this was unlikely to happen.

In 1767, Franklin visited France and was presented to the French king and queen, Louis XV and Maria Leszczynska. Observant as ever, he wrote to Mary Stevenson that the French ladies put rouge on their cheeks in artificial patterns. He talked with scientists and with people who studied trade and business. He came to feel that Britain, which made money from trade and manufacturing, might have very different interests from America. America would make its money from farming and developing its land.

Franklin traveled to Ireland as well. There he sided with the patriots fighting the British. They were watching the conflict between Britain and America with interest. Franklin saw the interests of Ireland and America as linked. He encouraged Americans to buy Irish linen even when they did not buy from the British in protest over British policies.

Fighting Charges Against Himself

Franklin finally found himself in trouble with the British government over some letters that were in his possession. They were written by Governor Thomas Hutchinson of Massachusetts and his brother-in-law, Andrew Oliver, to a minor member of the British government. In these letters, Hutchinson and Oliver criticized the colonial legislature. They said that the colonists should not have the same liberties as the English.

Franklin was secretive about how he had received the letters, but he sent them on to Thomas Cushing in Boston. Cushing was the speaker of the Massachusetts Assembly. Franklin thought they should be shown to others but not published. He may have wanted to let the colonists know what kind of reports the British were getting. When Samuel

Adams, a leading patriot, read the letters, he saw their value to the colonists' cause and had them published.

Back in England, the published letters stirred up a lot of questions for the British officials. How had the letters come to the Americans? Franklin wrote a letter to the newspapers saying that he was the one who had sent the letters to Boston. He did not say how he had obtained them. He had promised that the names of the people involved would be kept secret. He argued that he thought if the colonists knew that it was one of their own who had sent these reports to the British, then they would not blame the British legislature but would turn their anger on the people at home who wrote the letters. In fact, the Massachusetts legislature had asked that Governor Hutchinson and Andrew Oliver be removed from the offices they held.

The British government ordered Franklin to get a lawyer and appear before the Lord's Committee of His Majesty's Privy Council for Plantation Affairs. He was accused of stealing the letters in order to become the governor himself. Franklin, now sixty-eight years old, had to stand an hour and a half in the face of all these false charges. Franklin remained silent and at the end walked out in a calm manner. This tactic proved best. Later, he wrote out a defense, but it was not published until after his death.

The day after his appearance he received a letter telling him that he had been fired from his job as deputy postmaster general. This loss seemed to bother him more than all the accusations. He was proud of the way he had run the postal service.[17]

The enemies of an independent America came out even more strongly against Franklin. The accusations did not have any effect on his friends, who visited him the day after his ordeal. Back in the colonies, Benjamin Rush, one of the patriots, noted that this trial only increased Franklin's popularity. Rush hoped that Franklin would take no more British offices. If he did not, Franklin would be thought "among the first and greatest characters in the world."[18]

Franklin stayed in England, carrying on business

Franklin was examined by the House of Commons in 1766.

for the colonies for another year. In December of 1774, his wife, Deborah, died of a stroke. Franklin had not seen her since 1764 and did not even know that she was ill. With her death and with the end of his usefulness in England after the Hutchinson letters, he boarded a ship in 1775 to return to America. Franklin now began to think of himself as an American, rather than a British American.

6

SERVING HIS COUNTRY

When Ben Franklin stepped off the ship in Philadelphia on May 5, 1775, he was almost seventy years old. He learned of the bloodshed at Lexington and Concord, Massachusetts, on April 19, 1775. There American farmers had fired on British troops that had been sent to destroy arms and ammunition and to capture patriot leaders. This marked the beginning of the Revolutionary War. What could a man of his age contribute to his country? Apparently, a great deal.

Serving in the Second Continental Congress

The morning after his arrival, he was chosen to represent Pennsylvania in the Second Continental

Congress. The Congress was a gathering of delegates from the American colonies assembled to decide what to do about the relationship of the colonies to Britain. It was to meet in Philadelphia on May 10. Franklin was the oldest member of the Congress. Most of the other delegates were at least a generation younger, but he was much better known in Europe than they were. Some of the British said that he had gone home to start a rebellion because he was angry about the British trial against him.

Franklin tried to persuade his son, William, the governor of New Jersey, and his good friend, Governor Joseph Galloway of Pennsylvania, to give up their royal offices in order to support the efforts of the colonists. Neither man would do so because they remained loyal to Britain. Many families, including Franklin's, were split into loyalists (supporters of Britain) and patriots (fighters for independence).

The Congress put Franklin in charge of the postal service again. Also, he chaired the Committee of Safety designed to defend Pennsylvania. Franklin had to arm and train men to fight against the British. As a member of the committee to look after trade for the colonies, he had to find a way to get arms and ammunition while trying to cut trade with the British. He was also one of three assigned to take charge of the Native Americans living west of Pennsylvania and Virginia.

Franklin read to the Congress his *Articles of Confederation and Perpetual Union* that he had prepared some years before. In it he proposed that the colonies band together in a confederation—a government form that lets the individual member states retain much of their power. The Congress, as a whole, was not ready to move this far, and Franklin let it drop. Thomas Jefferson and some of the others, however, were ready to support his plan of uniting the colonies.

The Congress sent Franklin to Massachusetts to talk with General George Washington and various people in New England about the support of the inexperienced soldiers that would become the Continental Army. It was at this time that Abigail Adams met Franklin. She gave him a letter to take to her husband, John Adams, a member of Congress in Philadelphia. She reported to her husband about Franklin, "I found him social but not talkative, and when he spoke something useful dropped from his tongue. He was grave, yet pleasant and affable."[1]

On his return to Philadelphia, Franklin was given even more work to do for Congress. One of the most important tasks was the formation of a secret committee that was assigned the work of corresponding with friends abroad to win support for the patriot cause. It was the beginning of the American Department of State, which was in charge of foreign relations.

The French, Britain's enemy at the time, wanted to help the Americans in their fight against Britain, but they were cautious about doing so. They had to be sure that the Americans would really declare their independence from Great Britain. Yet the Americans could not declare independence with any hope of waging war against Britain without the support of arms from France.

In 1776, the Congress sent Franklin and three others to Canada to see if they could win the French Canadians to their cause. Canada at that time was also a colony of Britain, much like the American colonies. While the French Canadians did not care one way or the other about the American fight, their leaders were against joining with the Americans. At the time, they were content with British rule.

The trip to Canada and back was very hard. Franklin was tired and sick. They lived in frontier conditions—rowing up the Hudson River and staying in rustic inns or sleeping in the woods or on boats. April ice and snow blocked their progress. Franklin thanked a priest, John Carroll, for his care on the trip. Eight years later, an official of the Roman Catholic Church told Franklin that because of his praise for Carroll, the man would probably be made a bishop. Carroll later became the first archbishop in America.

Back home at last by June of 1776, Franklin felt worn out. It took him a while to get better. However, this man, now seventy years old, was back in Congress in time to play his part in the drafting and signing of the Declaration of Independence. An old friend from England, Lord Richard Howe, came over to represent the British and to see whether there was any chance to head off war. He met with Franklin, John Adams, and Edward Rutledge, all members of Congress. However, Howe arrived after the Declaration of Independence had been adopted, so there was little room for bargaining. Howe said that he would be as sorry if the American colonies went to war and lost as he would be for the loss of a brother.[2] Franklin replied that they would do all that they could to see that he would not have that sorrow.

Sir William Howe, Lord Richard Howe's brother, was the general of the British forces. Howe's troops attacked General George Washington, the patriot commander, and his troops in New York and drove him back. Nathan Hale, a patriot sent behind the lines on a mission for Washington, was caught and hanged as a spy. He said before his execution, "I only regret that I have but one life to lose for my country."[3] The Revolutionary War was on in earnest.

Benjamin Franklin, John Adams, and Edward Rutledge met Lord Richard Howe of England in 1776 in an attempt to work out a way of avoiding war.

Representing America in France

Congress secretly chose Franklin and two others to represent America in France. America did not seek a political alliance with France at this time but needed all the economic help France could give. Franklin slipped away with two of his grandsons, one seventeen years old, and the other seven. They boarded a ship with a cargo of indigo, a valuable plant used to make a blue dye. The indigo was to cover the expense of their secret mission. If their ship had been captured, Franklin would surely have been hanged for treason. Instead, the captain of their ship captured two British ships and brought them to France.

The journey was not easy for Franklin. He had not been feeling well since the trip to Canada. His health did not improve on board ship because he was not able to eat the fowl that was served. It was too tough on his teeth. When he landed in France, he still had a hard ride by carriage through a forest where robbers lurked.

The news of his arrival reached Paris before he did. There he was greeted as a hero because he represented America—a wilderness country. The French loved the idea of a simple, rustic life, if not the reality of it. Since America was seeking liberty—an idea in vogue at the time among teachers and writers, Franklin was very popular. Crowds tried to catch a glimpse of him when he went out. Small pictures of him were painted or printed and sold on the streets. He wrote his daughter that there were so many pictures of him that his face was as well known as that of the moon. Franklin may even have heightened this interest by moving out of Paris to a suburb and not going out often. The sightings of him were even more sensational after that.

Franklin realized the value of public support and even played up to it. He had worn his fur cap on his November sea trip to keep warm. When the French thought it a sign of an American scholar, Franklin kept wearing it. He wrote to a friend,

> Figure me in your mind as jolly as formerly and as strong and hearty, only a few years older; very plainly dressed, wearing my thin gray straight hair that peeps out under my only coiffure, a fine fur cap which comes down to my forehead almost to my spectacles. Think how this must appear among the powdered heads of Paris.[4]

The French wore powdered wigs and fancy dress. Franklin knew how to set himself apart.

Helping the War Effort from Abroad

Franklin's job in Paris was difficult. He had to win French support and money to aid the Americans. The news of British victories in the Revolutionary War was not good. A spy network was set in place by the British. Even one of his secretaries was an agent of England. Franklin knew he had spies all around. He just did not know who they were.

In the face of these problems, Franklin adopted a calm and patient manner. France wanted the Americans to win but was unwilling to risk siding with them if they were going to lose. Also, France wanted Spain to join her in supporting the Americans. Since Britain was the traditional enemy of both France and Spain, both countries would be better off as far as their land in the New World was concerned if the British did not have the American land as a base of attack.

The French official in charge of foreign policy, Charles Gravier, Comte de Vergennes, had to be careful. At first his king, Louis XVI, was not eager to support a rebellion against another king. The king had to be convinced that it would be in his own interest. Franklin did not press Vergennes too hard. Instead, Vergennes let Franklin win over the French crowds while he convinced the king.

The British watched every move the French made. They protested any act of public support by the French on behalf of the Americans. Much had to be done undercover. The French forbade ships to sail to America with arms, but then they did not prevent the ships from doing so.

The British Ambassador, David Murray, Viscount Storomont, claimed that the British had killed four thousand Americans and General Washington. When the French questioned Franklin about this report, he replied that the truth and what Storomont claimed were two different things. As a result of Franklin's comment, the people of Paris turned the name, Storomont, into slang for lying.

Franklin wrote for the press to tell America's side of the story. He continued writing letters to friends in Britain using false names to avoid the British spies. Franklin had to handle all sorts of offers from the people of Europe to help him and his country. In fact, he was swamped with visitors and letters.

He did play a role in sending to General Washington two very able officers—Marie Joseph, Marquis de Lafayette, and Friedrich Wilhelm, Baron von Steuben. Lafayette was a young Frenchman who became an aide to Washington. Von Steuben had good training as a Prussian (now German) officer. Franklin claimed von Steuben's rank was higher than it really was. He did this so Congress would accept another foreigner. Von Steuben helped Washington get his army into shape at Valley Forge.

Later, Franklin was asked by Congress to help with plans for an attack by sea on Britain. The American ships were commanded by John Paul Jones, a Scotsman who was to become an American Naval hero. The land forces, accompanying the sea attack, were to be led by Lafayette, who had proposed the plan. The land attack eventually had to be scrapped. However, Jones won the first major victory of the American Navy. His ship was named the *Bonhomme Richard*—French for "Poor Richard"—in honor of Franklin's almanac. Franklin was, in practice if not in name, the American secretary of the Navy on French soil.

Franklin was told that General Howe had captured Philadelphia. With his family and house there, this news must have worried Franklin. However, he replied, "I beg your pardon, Sir, Philadelphia has taken Howe."[5] It was a witty reply intended to reassure the French that he was not worried. Still, the news coming from America was not good. Often there were no letters that got through to him.

The British found that fighting a war so far from their shores was not easy. They had to pay soldiers from other countries to fight for them. The British offered a peace treaty that might have been accepted if it had come years earlier.

Slowly, the war began to favor the Americans. Now the French moved to give the Americans the treaty they sought. Franklin in his plain dress along with other Americans in fancy court dress were presented at court to Louis XVI, king of France. Of course, everyone looked at Franklin. The people around the king cheered the famous American.

Enjoying Life in France

During the eight and a half years that he lived in France, Franklin had no chance to travel outside Paris and the suburbs. When he had lived in England, he traveled often and found it restful. He had once said that it was a way of lengthening life. Two weeks of travel would seem like six months of living in one place because of the new sights.[6]

In his house in the suburbs of Paris, he lived with his grandsons until one was sent to a Swiss school. He kept in contact with his married daughter, Sarah Bache, and his four younger grandchildren in America as much as the wartime mail allowed. The

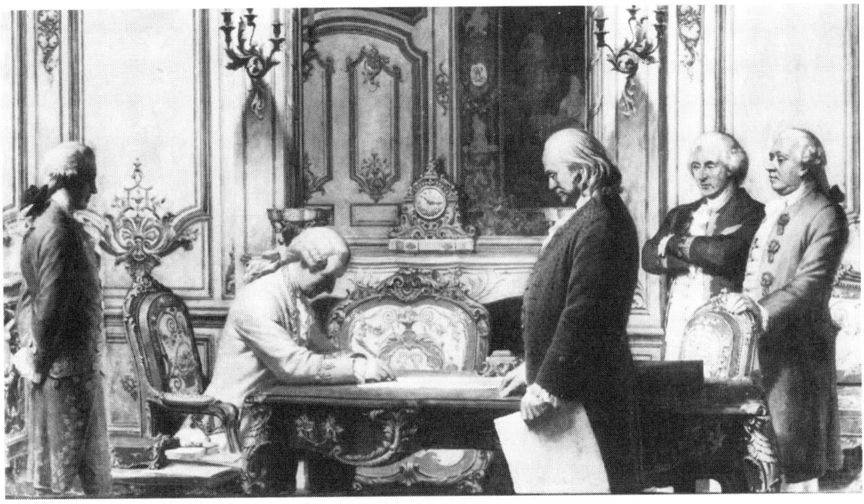

Benjamin Franklin, Silas Deane, and Richard Henry Lee look on as the French Vergennes signs a treaty that made France an ally of the United States in 1778.

British had occupied his house in Philadelphia in 1777 to 1778, and had carried off some of his musical instruments and electrical equipment. His daughter and her family returned to their house in Philadelphia when General Howe withdrew the British army.

Franklin made friends among his French neighbors and invited them to his home. He liked music and chess. He enjoyed the company of women and children and is even said to have proposed marriage to a French woman who turned him down. Also, Franklin liked to have around him a circle of friends with whom he could discuss the issues of the day. He was a member of the Freemasons (a benevolent secret society) and was active in a lodge in France.

Always the scientist, Franklin continued his study and experiments. He needed glasses but was upset because he needed two different types—one for reading, one for distance. He figured out a way of putting the two kinds of lenses together and invented bifocals.

Franklin also continued his career as a printer. He set up a press in his house. There he wrote and printed a number of pieces in both French and English.

The Americans had defeated the British at Saratoga (1777) and Yorktown (1781), thereby winning the war. This news amazed Franklin.[7] Franklin had a medal made to celebrate these two victories.

Franklin was sent to Paris to represent the United States in France. He was the best known American abroad and made new friends for the young nation.

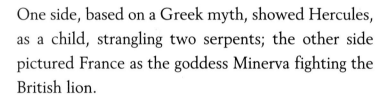

Baron Turgot's Praise of Franklin

In France, Baron Anne-Robert Turgot created a Latin saying about Franklin that translates: "He snatched the lightning from the heavens, the scepter from tyrants."[8] He focused on Franklin's work in inventing the lightning rod and in defeating George III of Britain. Franklin protested that the saying gave him too much credit—especially about the tyrants. The Revolutionary War was the work of many people. It was enough for him to have had a small share.

One side, based on a Greek myth, showed Hercules, as a child, strangling two serpents; the other side pictured France as the goddess Minerva fighting the British lion.

Winning the Peace

With the defeat of the British armies, America turned to Franklin to help with the peace. He was one of five men appointed by Congress to arrange a peace treaty. Again, Franklin faced a difficult task. Of the five men representing America, four were in Paris. Congress was far away. Since the mail took a long time to cross the ocean, the four often had to make judgments about what to do on their own, rather than write to Congress for advice. France, Spain, and the other powers of Europe were looking after their own interests. Franklin played a major role in drawing up the peace treaty by proposing many of the terms by which Britain gave up its rights in the United States. He signed it with the others and sent it off to Congress for approval.

A week before the signing, Franklin watched the first hydrogen gas balloon launched in Paris. Someone asked what good such balloons were. Franklin replied: "What good is a new-born baby?"[9] He speculated at how flight might change the world.

He now had time for writing about America. Franklin kept his printing press busy. He was interested in news coming from home. When he learned that the bald eagle had been chosen as a symbol for America, he was sorry. Franklin thought the eagle was a coward. Franklin preferred the turkey. According to Franklin, the turkey, though "vain and silly," would have the courage to attack a red-coated British soldier who might come into his "farmyard."[10]

With the war over, his son, William Franklin, who had supported the British, wrote to him. Franklin replied that he was glad that his son wanted to make peace. Franklin admitted that nothing had hurt him as much as his son's fighting against the American cause.[11]

However, Franklin was not pleased with the way William's son had turned out—he seemed to lack talent or ambition.[12] Franklin decided that his other grandson should learn a trade. He employed someone to teach the boy how to cast type for the printing press.

When Thomas Jefferson came from America to succeed Franklin as ambassador to France, the older man introduced his young colleague to his circle of friends. Jefferson greatly admired Franklin.[13] In many ways the two were alike, sharing a love of reading and an interest in science.

Returning Home in Triumph

At last on May 2, 1785, Congress released Franklin from his work in France. He was not sure that he would be able to stand the sea trip home. He was in a lot of pain from his illness. If he could not take the motion of the ship, he said he would have to be put ashore to die in Europe. The French said their good-byes with a gift from the king, a small picture of the king set with 408 diamonds. Franklin gave a gold snuffbox to the king's official in return.

Another ship from Europe beat his boat to Philadelphia. The news that Franklin would arrive soon meant that his friends had time to prepare a welcome. Everyone there was excited about his homecoming.[14] The cannons boomed out when he landed. Bells rang as he arrived at his home, where he met his daughter and the grandchildren he had never seen.

Franklin returned to America in September 1785. By October 29, he had been elected president of Pennsylvania. Now instead of the affairs of the world, Franklin focused on how best to govern his area. He did not neglect his love of science or his reading. He took long hot baths for relief of his pain in a copper tub shaped like a shoe. Franklin continued writing letters to friends abroad.

Franklin was not as upset with the way the states were linked under the Articles of Confederation as others were. Some wanted a closer union among the states with a stronger central government. However, Franklin hoped that good would come of the Constitutional Convention that had been called to design a better form of government.

Pennsylvania chose him as one of its delegates. Franklin's pet ideas were not accepted. He liked a single body—not two—in the legislature. He thought that having more than one chief executive would be good and that the executive officers should not be paid. Franklin helped the most by working out a compromise when members disagreed.

Even though Franklin did not agree with all aspects of the United States Constitution that the Constitutional Convention adopted, he backed it.

Independence Hall became the center of attention as the site of the debates and meetings that produced the Constitution of the United States.

He and the other delegates signed it on September 17, 1787. As others walked up to sign, Franklin pointed to the president's chair. It had a sun painted on it. He is reported to have said,

> I have often . . . in the course of this session . . . looked at that . . . without being able to tell whether it was rising or setting; but now at length I have the happiness to know that it is a rising and not a setting sun.[15]

As Franklin left the building, a lady called out, "Dr. Franklin, what kind of government did you give us? A monarchy or a republic?" She wanted to know if the country would be ruled by a king or president and legislature?

Franklin shouted back, "A republic, if you can keep it!"[16] Republics are harder for citizens to keep than monarchies, for citizens of republics must make choices.

Always thinking about the world, Franklin wrote a friend in France about the Constitutional Convention. If it succeeded, Franklin suggested that the nations of Europe form a union among themselves as the American states had done.

Franklin lived long enough to get just the early news of the French Revolution, which overturned the king there. He worried about the fate of his French friends. However, he supported strongly the need for more recognition of the rights of the people.

One of the last public issues that Franklin wrote

about was slavery. Although he had owned and sold slaves, he had long favored doing away with slavery. Now with less than a month to live, he wrote a piece comparing American slavery with Algerian slavery of Christians. In the article, his wit was as good as in any piece he wrote in his youth.

One of Franklin's last visitors was Thomas Jefferson, who had returned from France to become

Franklin's Epitaph

When Franklin was about twenty-one years old, he wrote this for his tomb:

The body of
B. Franklin, Printer
(Like the Cover of an Old Book
Its Contents Torn Out
And Stript of its Lettering and Gilding)
Lies Here, Food for Worms,
But the Work shall not be Lost;
For it will (as he Believ'd) Appear once More
In a New and More Elegant Edition
Revised and Corrected
By the Author.[17]

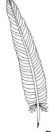

It was not used as his epitaph, however. Franklin's will directed the use of "Benjamin and Deborah Franklin: 1790" on the tombstone.

secretary of state. He brought news of friends. Jefferson was the only American outside Franklin's family to receive a copy of part of the autobiography that Franklin had written.

A while before his death, Franklin had written to George Washington that he had spent the last two years in great pain. Still he was glad to have lived those years because he had seen the forming of the new United States government with Washington as its first president.

Several days before his death, Franklin began to feel a pain in his chest and have difficulty breathing. He was cared for by his daughter, Sarah Bache, and spent time with her seven children. Two of his grandsons were with him when he died quietly on April 17, 1790, at the age of eighty-four.

Franklin's funeral, on April 21, was a great public event. All the religious leaders of the city walked before the coffin. Important political and business leaders carried the coffin. An estimated twenty thousand people saw the funeral. He was buried at the Christ Church graveyard in Philadelphia, beside his wife, Deborah, and son, Francis. At his funeral, the militia that he had organized and had been colonel of fired guns in salute. In France, his friends voted to hold a three-day period of mourning for him.

7

Giving Us A Hero

From the Declaration of Independence to the Constitution of the United States, Benjamin Franklin was an important hero for Americans. He was a leader at home and represented his country abroad in Europe.

His talents and fame are not limited to one realm.[1] Franklin was a scientist, an inventor, a businessman, a politician, and an ambassador. He not only created things but also suggested ways to make his city and his world work better.

From his childhood on, Franklin took responsibility for his life. Out on his own at an early age, he

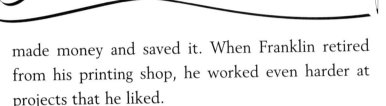

President Truman's Words About Franklin

"I don't think that Franklin has found his real place in American history yet—he was one of the great ones of his time and of all American history."

—President Harry Truman[2]

made money and saved it. When Franklin retired from his printing shop, he worked even harder at projects that he liked.

Though Benjamin Franklin achieved fame for discovering electricity in lightning, he was also a prolific inventor. He invented many things, including: bifocals, a way of getting salt out of salt water, lightning rods, a stove, a copying machine, a chair that folded into a stepladder, and a mirror that was used to check who was at the door.

He was ahead of his time with many of his ideas: wanting slavery abolished, prisons reformed, supporting efforts to establish a Northwest Passage between the Atlantic and the Pacific, and bringing the first bathtub to America. He also translated the Bible into ordinary English, started writing editorials and cartoons in newspapers, organized a fire department, set up a hospital that is still in operation, and planned a medical school. Some of Franklin's other contributions include: building the

Franklin was one of our first heroes. His life still inspires us to excel in many different fields. His actions to bring about liberty for all are still an example for us.

Benjamin Franklin is honored as an American hero. His portrait appears on the $100 bill.

first second-story toilet, setting up a library, helping start the American Navy, and publishing the first novel in America. Franklin even became the first windsurfer by using kites to pull him while he floated on a lake. He thought of using paratroopers and submarines in warfare. Franklin considered life on other planets likely and space infinite. He wrote a soap opera for his *Poor Richard's Almanac* and knew fruit, fresh air, and exercise were necessary for good health.

Is it any wonder that Benjamin Franklin wanted to see what the world would be like two or three centuries after he lived?[3] Once, he watched as some flies that appeared to be drowned in wine were brought back to life in the sun. He wished that he could be put in a cask of wine to come back to life centuries later! He wanted to observe the state of America in a hundred years.[4] What do you think Benjamin Franklin would think of the United States of America today?

CHRONOLOGY

1706—Born on January 17 in Boston.

1718—Goes to work for his brother, James, in printing shop.

1723—Runs away to Philadelphia.

1724—Sails to London to study latest developments in printing.

1726—Returns to Philadelphia.

1729—Sets up his newspaper, the *Pennsylvania Gazette*.

1732—Publishes his *Poor Richard's Almanac*.

1737—Appointed postmaster of Philadelphia.

1748—Retires from printing business.

1752—Conducts lightning experiment with kite.

1756—Elected to Royal Society of Britain.

1757—Goes to London as agent for Pennsylvania legislature.

1762—Returns to Philadelphia.

1764—Sent back to London as colonial agent.

1772—Elected to French Academy of Science.

1775—Returns to America; Elected to Second Continental Congress.

1776—Assists in drafting of and signs Declaration of Independence; Sails for France as representative of Congress.

1782—Signs the preliminary peace treaty with Britain.

1783—Participates in planning Treaty of Paris between Britain (on one side) and the United States, France, Spain, and the Netherlands (on the other side) that officially ended the Revolutionary War.

1785—Returns to America; Elected president of Pennsylvania and member of Constitutional Convention.

1787—Signs the Constitution of the United States.

1790—Dies on April 17 at the age of eighty-four.

Chapter Notes

Chapter 1

1. Alfred Owen Aldridge, *Benjamin Franklin: Philosopher & Man* (Philadelphia: J. B. Lippincott, 1965), p. 261.

2. Dumas Malone, *The Story of the Declaration of Independence* (New York: Oxford University Press, 1954), p. 85.

3. Ibid., pp. 91–92.

4. James C. Humes, *The Wit & Wisdom of Benjamin Franklin: A Treasury of More Than 900 Quotations and Anecdotes* (New York: HarperCollins Publishers, 1995), p. 71.

5. Malone, p. 69.

6. P. M. Zall, *Ben Franklin Laughing: Anecdotes from Original Sources by and about Benjamin Franklin* (Berkeley: University of California Press, 1980), pp. 137–138.

7. Humes, p. 167.

Chapter 2

1. P. M. Zall, *Ben Franklin Laughing: Anecdotes from Original Sources by and about Benjamin Franklin* (Berkeley: University of California Press, 1980), p. 113.

2. Ibid., pp. 42–43.

3. Benjamin Franklin, *The Autobiography of Benjamin Franklin* (Boston: Houghton Mifflin Co., 1886), p. 15. written by him at various times, 1771, 1784, and 1788, and published after his death.

4. Ibid., pp. 17–18.

5. Zall, p. 118.
6. Franklin, p. 28.

Chapter 3

1. Benjamin Franklin, *The Autobiography of Benjamin Franklin* (Boston: Houghton Mifflin Co., 1886), p. 48.
2. Ibid., p. 33.
3. Ibid.
4. Ibid., p. 56.
5. Ibid., p. 57.
6. Ibid.
7. Ibid., p. 58.
8. Ibid., p. 59.
9. Ibid., p. 60.
10. Ibid., p. 61.
11. James C. Humes, *The Wit & Wisdom of Benjamin Franklin: A Treasury of More Than 900 Quotations and Anecdotes* (New York: HarperCollins Publishers, 1995), pp. 24, 21, 31, 41, 58, and 67.

Chapter 4

1. Benjamin Franklin, *The Autobiography of Benjamin Franklin* (Boston: Houghton Mifflin Co., 1886), p. 70.
2. Ibid., p. 71.
3. *The Oxford Dictionary of Quotations*, 3rd ed. (Oxford: Oxford University Press, 1979), p. 218.
4. Franklin, p. 83.
5. Ibid., p. 87.
6. Claude-Anne Lopez and Eugenia W. Herbert, *The Private Franklin: The Man and His Family* (New York: W. W. Norton & Company, Inc., 1975), pp. 22–23.
7. Ibid., p. 24.
8. Franklin, p. 101.

9. Ibid., pp. 101–102.
10. Ibid., p. 107.
11. Ibid., p. 108.
12. Ibid., pp. 102–103.
13. Ibid., pp. 120–121.
14. Ibid., pp. 123–124.

Chapter 5

1. Benjamin Franklin, *The Autobiography of Benjamin Franklin* (Boston: Houghton Mifflin Co., 1886), p. 199.
2. Albert Henry Smyth, *The Writings of Benjamin Franklin* (New York: Macmillan Company, 1905–07), vol. 3, pp. 32–35.
3. Joseph Priestley, *History and Present State of Electricity*, 2d ed. (London: J. Dodsley, 1769), pp. 171–172.
4. Lois M. MacLaurin, *Franklin's Vocabulary* (Garden City, 1928), pp. 57–76, quoted in Carl Van Doren, *Benjamin Franklin* (New York: Viking Press, 1938), p. 173.
5. Thomas Fleming, *The Man Who Dared the Lightning: A New Look at Benjamin Franklin* (New York: William Morrow and Company, 1971), p. 10.
6. Franklin, p. 154.
7. Ibid., p. 183.
8. Ibid., p. 215.
9. Ibid., p. 230.
10. Ibid.
11. Ibid.
12. Claude-Anne Lopez and Eugenia W. Herbert, *The Private Franklin: The Man and His Family* (New York: W. W. Norton & Company, Inc., 1975), p. 98.
13. Van Doren, pp. 300, 303.

14. Benjamin Franklin, *Narratives of the Late Massacres in Lancaster County,* in Albert Henry Smyth, *The Writings of Benjamin Franklin* (New York: Macmillan Company, 1905–07), vol. 4, pp. 289–314.

15. Lopez and Herbert, pp. 127–128.

16. Van Doren, p. 352.

17. Catherine Drinker Bowen, *The Most Dangerous Man in America: Scenes from the Life of Benjamin Franklin* (Boston: Little Brown and Company, 1974), pp. 241–242.

18. Ibid., p. 243.

19. Ibid., p. 246.

Chapter 6

1. Bernard Fay, *Franklin, The Apostle of Modern Times* (Boston: Little, Brown and Company, 1929), p. 390.

2. Ibid., p. 559.

3. *The Oxford Dictionary of Quotations*, 3rd ed. (Oxford: Oxford University Press, 1979), p. 237.

4. Frank Donovan, *The Benjamin Franklin Papers* (New York: Dodd, Mead & Company, 1962), p. 183.

5. Thomas Fleming, *The Man Who Dared the Lightning: A New Look at Benjamin Franklin* (New York: William Morrow and Company, 1971), p. 371.

6. Carl Van Doren, *Benjamin Franklin* (New York: Viking Press, 1938), p. 370.

7. Ibid., p. 628.

8. Alfred Owen Aldridge, *Franklin and His French Contemporaries* (New York: New York University Press, 1957), p. 16.

9. Ibid., p. 188.

10. Van Doren, pp. 708–709.

11. Robert Middlekauff, *Benjamin Franklin and His Enemies* (Berkeley: University of California Press, 1996), pp. 208–209, 212.

12. William Sterne Randall, *A Little Revenge: Benjamin Franklin and His Son* (Boston: Little Brown and Company, 1984), p. 492.

13. Dumas Malone, *Jefferson and the Rights of Man* (Boston: Little Brown and Company, 1951), p. 34.

14. Fleming, p. 480.

15. Ibid., p. 486.

16. Humes, p. 218.

17. Esmond Wright, ed., *Benjamin Franklin: His Life As He Wrote It* (Cambridge, Mass.: Harvard University Press, 1990), pp. 274–275.

Chapter 7

1. Many of the records are detailed in the book by Humes.

2. Thomas Fleming, *The Man Who Dared the Lightning: A New Look at Benjamin Franklin* (New York: William Morrow and Company, 1971), p. xi.

3. James C. Humes, *The Wit & Wisdom of Benjamin Franklin: A Treasury of More Than 900 Quotations and Anecdotes* (New York: HarperCollins Publishers, 1995), p. xiv.

4. Carl Van Doren, *Benjamin Franklin* (New York: Viking Press, 1938), p. 431.

Glossary

Articles of Confederation—Constitution of the thirteen American states, adopted in 1781 but replaced in 1788 by the Constitution of the United States.

Bonhomme Richard—Ship of John Paul Jones named in French after Franklin's *Poor Richard's Almanac*.

Continental Congress—Two legislative sessions: the first, in 1774, complained to Britain about what was being done to Americans; the second, from 1775 to 1789, adopted the Declaration of Independence and set up the Articles of Confederation.

Declaration of Independence—Document in which the Second Continental Congress on July 4, 1776, declared the thirteen American colonies independent of Britain.

Junto—Club devoted to discussion of issues, started by Franklin and other businessmen.

loyalists—Colonists who remained loyal to Britain in the Revolutionary War.

Moravians—Group of people from the central part of eastern Europe who settled on the frontier in Pennsylvania.

patriots—Colonists who supported independence in the Revolutionary War.

Poor Richard's Almanac—Annual book published by Franklin and called Poor Richard's after a character he invented named Richard Saunders.

Quakers—Nickname for the Society of Friends, a religious group that settled in Pennsylvania.

Revolutionary War—The war between Britain and the thirteen American colonies from 1775 to 1783 by which the colonies won independence.

Silence Dogood—Female name Franklin used when he wrote a series of articles for his brother's paper.

Stamp Act—Legislation passed by Britain in 1765 to raise money by requiring colonists to buy stamps for important legal papers, newspapers, and even playing cards; repealed in 1766.

Further Reading

Franklin, Benjamin. *The Autobiography of Benjamin Franklin*. Boston: Houghton Mifflin Co., 1886. (This has been reprinted in various editions.)

Hall, Robert Lee. *Benjamin Franklin Takes the Case*. New York: St. Martin's Press, 1988. (This is the first book in a series of adult mystery novels. In this fictional series, Benjamin Franklin is a detective. The stories take place in eighteenth-century London.)

Hawke, David Freeman. *Franklin: What Manner of Man*. New York: Harper & Row, 1976, (Recorded Books, 1988). (This is an adult biography of Franklin on audiotape.)

Kent, Deborah. *The American Revolution: "Give Me Liberty or Give Me Death."* Springfield, NJ: Enslow Publishers, Inc., 1994.

INDEX